T0328575

Cambridge Elements ≡

Elements in Women Theatre Makers
edited by
Elaine Aston
Lancaster University
Melissa Sihra
Trinity College Dublin

EMMA RICE'S FEMINIST ACTS OF LOVE

Lisa Peck
University of Sussex

CAMBRIDGE
UNIVERSITY PRESS

Shaftesbury Road, Cambridge CB2 8EA, United Kingdom

One Liberty Plaza, 20th Floor, New York, NY 10006, USA

477 Williamstown Road, Port Melbourne, VIC 3207, Australia

314–321, 3rd Floor, Plot 3, Splendor Forum, Jasola District Centre,
New Delhi – 110025, India

103 Penang Road, #05–06/07, Visioncrest Commercial, Singapore 238467

Cambridge University Press is part of Cambridge University Press & Assessment,
a department of the University of Cambridge.

We share the University's mission to contribute to society through the pursuit of
education, learning and research at the highest international levels of excellence.

www.cambridge.org
Information on this title: www.cambridge.org/9781009287227

DOI: 10.1017/9781009287234

First published 2023

A catalogue record for this publication is available from the British Library.

ISBN 978-1-009-28722-7 Paperback
ISSN 2634-2391 (online)
ISSN 2634-2383 (print)

Emma Rice's Feminist Acts of Love

Elements in Women Theatre Makers

DOI: 10.1017/9781009287234
First published online: June 2023

Lisa Peck
University of Sussex

Author for correspondence: Lisa Peck, lisa.peck@sussex.ac.uk

Abstract: This is a love story but not as you know it. Should an academic study be framed in this way? Love seems an unlikely bedfellow for critical thinking. Watching an Emma Rice production and being in her rehearsal room you feel the love: a warm and generous welcoming in, a joyful celebration of the theatrical exchange. What produces this pleasurable affect and how might we consider its political potential?

This Element positions Emma's theatre-making, a body of work spanning three decades, as feminist acts of love. Drawing on fieldwork research, her practice is viewed through the critical lenses of feminisms and affect to consider its contextual tensions, its ethics of affirmation, staging of femininities and contribution to queer worldmaking. Mapping her work from this perspective brings to light her important contribution to UK feminist theatre, its love activism offering an emergent strategy for change.

Keywords: Emma Rice, theatre directing, feminisms, affect, queer worldmaking

ISBNs: 9781009287227 (PB), 9781009287234 (OC)
ISSNs: 2634-2391 (online), 2634-2383 (print)

Contents

1 Introduction: Feminisms, Feeling and Love

This is a love story but not as you know it.

Should an academic study be framed in this way? Love seems an unlikely bedfellow for critical thinking. In this Element, I think about Emma Rice's work, a body of theatre-making spanning three decades, as feminist acts of love.

It is the summer of 2022 and the latest series of *Love Island* has just ended. On this 'vote-em-off' reality TV show singletons frolic together in the sun, hoping to find 'the one'. The romantic love story is a mainstay of culture, from popular entertainment to opera, a pervasive obsession spearing the heart of the humanist dream. Looking outside of the bourgeoisie couple and the nuclear family love takes other forms (vocational, friendship, kinship, public, queer, non-human, sensual, spiritual, and erotic). Here, I work with love as a force for feminist activism.

I first started to explore Emma's work in 2008, looking at feminist theatre-making practices in the United Kingdom (Peck, 2021). In developing my thinking, I draw on three in-depth interviews with Emma, interviews with seven collaborators, fieldwork (a total of fourteen days rehearsal observation, including two productions, two research and development processes and a summer school), archival material, live and digital productions, journalistic reviews and feminist scholarship.[1] My research methodology is a tripartite exchange between myself as researcher, Emma, and the practitioners (in particular actors) with whom she works. Wherever possible I give space to the practitioners' voices.

I trouble academic tradition as my own feminist act. Rather than refer to the main protagonist by her surname, which, to my mind, un-genders, depersonalises and reaffirms hierarchies – all antithetical to my intentions – she is Emma throughout. My preference calls attention to what and how this convention performs. Why have we come to decide that using a surname bestows authority or critical distance? My approach to writing about the work of a live practitioner is relational, a generous passing between, my own act of love, critical *and* loving. Emma wouldn't refer to me as Peck. I do, however, maintain academic convention with other sources.

At the time of writing, between 1999 and 2022, Emma has made thirty-one productions, the majority exploring love – romantic, familial, friendship, non-human, and artistic.[2] These love stories, told from a female perspective, don't

---

[1] This fieldwork took place between June and October 2022. Three one hour interviews with Emma took place over three weeks in June/July 2022 via Zoom. Individual interviews with collaborators were mainly face to face.

[2] Her body of work is listed in the Appendix, where I highlight and cross-reference productions that have received close analysis in this Element. For access to Emma's work, see Wise Children at www.wisechildrendigital.com/, Shakespeare's Globe https://player.shakespearesglobe.com/ and the National Theatre archive www.nationaltheatre.org.uk/about-us/archive/.

shy away from vicissitudes – pain is intertwined with pleasure, joy with despair – in an emotional scramble for freedom, hope and the possibility of happiness. Her storytelling is dominated by adaptations: myths, folk tales and legends, such as *The Red Shoes* (2002), *The Bacchae* (2005), *Tristan and Yseult* (2006) and *The Wild Bride* (2011); popular novels, such as Angela Carter's *Wise Children* (2018), Enid Blyton's *Mallory Towers* (2019) and Charlotte Bronte's *Wuthering Heights* (2021); and iconic films/television, such as *Brief Encounter* (2009), *The Umbrellas of Cherbourg* (2012), *Steptoe and Son* (2012) and *Bagdad Café* (2021). Alongside these adaptations are productions of Shakespeare, freely adapted such as *Cymbeline* (2007), or close-to-the-text, such as *A Midsummer Night's Dream* (2016) and *Twelfth Night* (2017); operatic productions, such as *Orpheus in the Underworld* with English National Opera (2019) and new writing, such as Tanika Gupta's *The Empress* with the Royal Shakespeare Company (2013). The extent to which a work emerges through an ensemble devising process starts with the original text, or Emma's own adaptation will depend on the nature and scale of the production. Inherent in the process of adaptation is potential political affect. When audiences come to see a stage adaptation of a story they have already encountered, whether intimately familiar or remotely aware of the original, they bring preconceptions. Through the iteration Emma invites us to view the story we thought we knew in a different way, from a different perspective or with an unexpected turn of events. For example, in her adaptation of *Wuthering Heights*, it is the invented chorus of the personified Yorkshire Moor (not Nelly Dean) that narrates and comments on the epic love story; in *Don John*, an adaptation of Mozart's Don Giovani, the story is told from the perspective of John's female victims who enact their revenge; in Emma's adaptation of Hans Christian Anderson's *The Red Shoes*, the central protagonist, Lydia, rather than embrace forgiveness and welcome death as just punishment for her transgression, fights off the supposedly benevolent angel, refusing death, to go 'her own way' (Babbage, 2018, pp. 96–7). Emma's adapting practice subverts popular stories, making space to rethink preconceptions and to question value systems.

Her work is complicated by her gendered position, which splits opinions and causes controversy. She has been variously described by critics as 'the most relentlessly inventive British theatre director of the twenty-first century' (Cavendish, 2018) and the 'conundrum of British theatre' (Simpson, 2022). Whilst she has been lauded with awards – in 2019 winning the Outstanding Contribution to British Theatre at the UK Theatre Awards, and in 2022 chosen by Sky Arts as one of the fifty most influential British artists of all time – it is curious that her important feminist body of work has not been recognised in scholarship.[3] And yet, she is one of a handful of women in this century to forge a lifetime career in UK theatre: building a company, advancing regional touring and launching a school to develop young talent. To my mind, Emma's determined commitment to nurturing a theatre family sits within a constellation of radical practitioners such as Annabel Arden, co-founder of Complicité, Anne Jellicoe (1927–) and her development of the community play, Annie Castledine (1939–2016) and Joan Littlewood (1914–2002), described as 'The Mother of Modern Theatre' (BBC News, 2002).

Emma's gender has performed itself very publicly. In 2007, the then artistic director of The National Theatre, Nicolas Hytner, defended her and other women theatre directors from the misogynistic bias of British theatre critics (*The Guardian*, 2007). The debate drew attention to the gendered hierarchies of the industry and the ways that women's freedom as artists was more critically held to account. In 2016, Emma became the first female artistic director of one of the most iconic theatre spaces in the world, Shakespeare's Globe, a reconstruction of an Elizabethan playhouse on the South Bank in London. The tenure, which should have been for five years, was cut short after two successful seasons due to irreconcilable differences with the executive board who 'took exception to her experimental style' (Singh, 2017). Again, this public ousting drew attention to the ways that Emma and her work were positioned in the cultural industry, where certain belittling discriminations worked against her: her gender, being seen to be a female auteur, making popular theatre, messing with the classics, presenting herself as anti-intellectual, making work that is local *and* global, commercial *and* experimental, work that unapologetically evokes emotion (sentimentality, empathy, pain and pleasure) through love stories – a potent cocktail which I position as feminist activism. In Section 2, I map her theatre journey and its feminisms in relation to reductive contextual binaries (the individual *or* the group, text *or* performance, the radical *or* the popular). These binaries cut to the heart of tensions in the UK theatre industry and in the academy.

Returning to the title of this Element, what do I mean by feminist acts of love? What are the critical lenses that underpin my thinking about feminisms, feeling, and love?

1.1 Feminisms

Feminism is a slippery term that can easily become a contested category rather than a way of being in the world. In relation *with* Emma's work, I turn to the posthuman feminism of Rosi Braidotti. Braidotti locates her project firmly in

---

[3] Duška Radosavljević's scholarship on Kneehigh has had the largest impact and is referenced throughout.

the present moment and what feminism can do in the here-and-now to seek a more nuanced position, with an emphasis on redefining humanism. This recognises the blurring of the social, radical and liberal feminist movements, eclipsed by new concerns.[4] Feminism for the twenty-first century is not only a struggle for equality of all marginal communities, including people of colour, Black, indigenous peoples and LGBTQ+, but also looks beyond human to imagine other ways of becoming human and being in the world, embodied and embedded, 'a heterogeneous assemblage' (Braidotti, 2022, p. 125). Braidotti seeks to mobilise feminism's radical politics into action.

Posthuman feminism has developed from new materialisms that foreground processes of becoming and relationality – the sexuate nature of being and nature/culture *besideness* (the mutual reliance on human and non-human). Realising the need for a posthuman convergence is a necessary response to seismic shifts in cultural, social and planetary conditions – structural injustice, unequal distribution of wealth, environmental crisis and technological develop-ments. This builds on ecofeminism, LGBTQ+ and critical race theories and feminist technoscience. For Braidotti, a posthuman feminist agenda has the potential to shape an affirmative relational ethics for change, which, like Jill Dolan's utopian theatre, constructs horizons for hope, decolonial and antiracist, where '"We"-who-are-not-one-and-the-same-but-are-in-*this*-together' (Braidotti, 2022, p.8). Braidotti's code word for this is 'transversality', which works from an ethics of affirmation as transformative feminist practice (Braidotti, 2022, p. 103). I enjoy thinking through this aspect of Emma's practice throughout this Element.

Her work's hybrid style, defying easy categorisation but with a distinct theatrical language, ignites transversal potential. It has been described as folk theatre, poor theatre and total theatre with a punk aesthetic, characterised by exuberant theatricality. Quentin Letts writes: 'That is the appeal of an Emma Rice show: the whole thing is so dolloped with theatrical bombast, so suffused with warmth, it finally melts you into submission' (2018). Whilst total theatre recognises multi-disciplined storytelling, harnessing the whole apparatus of theatricality and stagecraft – acting, song, dance, text, set, costume, lights, sound, puppets, digital – it falls short as a definition for Emma's work as it doesn't attend to its politics, its transversal effect on an audience. Emma herself resists these definitions, describing its theatrical style as 'patchwork' or 'tapes-try' (Rice, 2022a). I'm interested in digging into the feminist potential of this

---

[4] I lean here on Elaine Aston's *Restaging Feminisms*, which maps the evolution of radical, socialist and liberal feminisms in UK theatre (Aston, 2020). Radical feminism sees the patriarchy as the main obstacle; socialist feminism foregrounds class politics; liberal feminism, 'a strategy' rather than a movement, pursues women's advancement through existing systems (2020, p. 7).

metaphor. In Section 3, I seek out the transversal, through fieldwork observation and interviews, to position her work as theatre of assemblage, shaping a feminist politics through its form, process of construction and affect.

In posthuman feminism, where relational transversality is at the heart of the project, we come into being in relation *with*. So, posthuman feminism foregrounds relational ethics and cross-species interdependence – a middle ground, or imminence – working with a decolonial, multispecies, feminist ecology (Braidotti, 2022, p. 100). Whilst feminist technoscience calls for a critical 'de-naturalisation' of the body, ecofeminism and feminist materialism propose 'strategic re-naturalisation' (Braidotti, 2022, pp.107 39). At this time of cultural, social and ecological crisis, the body necessarily experiences a 'double pull towards re-materialisation and de-materialisation' in relation to 'human and non-human entities' (Braidotti, 2022, p. 111). These strands operate *beside* each other to converge, recognising that cells and genomes are, nodding to Karen Barad (2003), in constant diffraction, to regenerate and re-naturalise the artificial, 'Naturalising queerness, queering nature' (Braidotti, 2022, p. 176). I see this position reflected in the representation of gender in Emma's works. In Section 4, I examine her exploration of femaleness, drawing on interviews and key productions: *The Wild Bride* and *Don John*. In Section 5, through the analyses of *The Bacchae*, *A Midsummer Night's Dream* and *Wise Children*, I consider queering strategies as political activism where 'Difference is recast as trans individual complexity, or the principle of not one' (Braidotti, 2022, p. 177).

1.2 Feelings

An 'Emma Rice show' is unapologetically emotional. It does things to your body; you get goosebumps, the hairs on your arms stand on end, a surge of adrenaline stimulating miniscule muscles that pull at the hair roots. Her ability to affect bodies with the extremes of emotion through theatrical storytelling defines her work, which has led me to work with theoretical frameworks of affect *in relationship with* feminism throughout this Element.

Whilst she doesn't explicitly refer to affect theory, Braidotti does identify carnal empiricism – the idea that knowledge is a felt sense, experienced through and passed between bodies – as the methodology for posthuman feminism (2022, p. 107). Throughout the Element I position Emma's work as theatre of affect, focussing on the ways it produces feelings – particularly feelings of happiness, empathy and sentimentality through love.

To amplify considerations of affect at this introductory stage, it is useful to note how Melissa Gregory and Gregory Seigworth, in *The Affect Theatre*

Reader, overview the multiple variations of affect theory and its refusal to be pinned down (2010). Affect, they observe, has an assortment of 'philosophical/ psychological/physiological underpinnings, critical vocabularies, and onto-logical pathways, and, thus, can be (and has been) turned toward all manner of political/pragmatic/performative ends' (Braidotti, 2022, p. 4). For my pur-poses, I am drawn to approaches that pay attention to affect's in-between spaces as potentially transformative: its capacity to act and be acted upon, underpinned by the Deleuzian concern with immanence (2005) and Spinoza's relational ethics (1996). This can be discerned in feminist work that looks beyond fixed categories to the sticky and blurred spaces of imminence, between limitations of gender (Elizabeth Grosz 1994; Moira Gatens 1996; Rosi Braidotti, 2022) or human and non-human (Karen Barad, 2003; Jane Bennet, 2010; Donna Haraway, 2016). These ribbons of critical feminist affect are threaded through-out sections, highlighting the feeling strategies operating in the in-between spaces of Emma's work.

In *Theatre and Feeling*, Erin Hurley identifies three key feeling strategies – affect, emotion and mood – to interrogate the ways in which feelings come to matter in systems of cultural value. Affects are biological reactions, triggered through our nervous systems, producing felt bodily changes – for example sweating, heart beating faster, breathing changing and goosebumps. According to Hurley, as automatic responses, affects indicate our base 'animal nature'. Emotion is the perception of those physiological affects, involving judgement or discernment, more complex and socially inscribed, such as shame or love (2010, p. 16). Emotion, as a cultural/social construction acts as 'a bridge between body and mind, between sensation and evaluation, and indeed between individual and group. ... Emotion is conventionalised or codified affect, fitted into meanings in an intersubjective context' (Hurley, 2010, p. 19). Mood is a disposition or ambient, background state. It creates rhythms and resonance that initiate particular feelings. Each category of feeling operates as 'feeling technologies' and moves us, shifting how we experience and make sense of the world. Hurley problematises the way that popular culture, which offers 'feeling-labour', falls into dichotomies and hierarchies of value: high culture above low culture, thought above feeling, reason above emotion, serious above comedy, education above entertainment, mind above body, human above animal, male above female, White above Black. I point to these systems of control in Section 2. The transformational promise of affect lies in its processual nature – it's 'what-if-ness'? And, as such, this makes affect a vital material in theatre. Consequently, the ways that Emma's work produces feeling is central to its feminist activism – activism that I suggest is founded on love.

1.3 Love

Figure 1 Emma Rice and Don Jamieson in *The Birthday Party* (1992) dir. Nikki Sved (renamed *The Flying Lovers of Vitebsk* in 2016)

Photo courtesy of Leah Gordon

Emma talks a lot about love. She doesn't shy away from using the word to explain her work, her practice, her life choices. This image, taken early in her career, captures her performing a heartrending love story with her then husband. Her personal life has been inextricably entwined with her practice. She reflects, 'I have always been very good at falling in love. Love pours out of me quite messily, passionately and unstoppably. But this "talent" has also got me in deep trouble. Love is grown up, difficult and damaging stuff. It is about your responsibility for another human being, as well as your responsibility to your own bursting soul' (Rice, 2022). In this Element I suggest that, for Emma, love is *the* life force of life and art.

This is not limited to romantic love. Theatre and theatre-making have their foundations in constructs of love. Theatre people explain why they do what they do with a variation of the theme of love; amateur in French translates as 'lover'; Antonin Artaud's claims 'the actor is an athlete of the heart' (Hurley, 2010, p. 5). In theatre, acts of love, or 'feeling-labour', can be seen as social work, as audiences come to rethink how to be in the world together through shared feeling (Hurley, 2010, p. 4).

I come to an understanding of love through the scholarship of bell hooks. Her love trilogy charts her journey to position love as personal creed and political activism. The essential drive towards love as the ultimate solution is bound by its failure. hooks' definition of love is drawn from M. Scott Peck's *The Road Less Travelled* (1978), where he defines love as 'the will to extend oneself for the purpose of nurturing one's own or another's spiritual growth' (hooks, 2000, p. 5). For hooks, this looks beyond romantic love:

> [W]hen we see love as the will to nurture one's own or another's spiritual growth, revealed through acts of care, respect, knowing, and assuming responsibility, the foundation of all love in our life is the same. There is no special love exclusively reserved for romantic partners. Genuine love is the foundation of our engagement with ourselves, with family, with friends, with partners, with everyone we choose to love. (hooks, 2000, p. 136)

hooks' work sits within Black feminist love politics. For Jenifer Nash, this activism looks beyond identity and intersectionality towards a practice that can transcend limitations of selfhood. She overviews the development of second-wave Black feminist love politics from the South (Alice Walker, 1983; Audre Lorde, 1984; June Jordan, 2003) as being bound up with self-love as a practice of freedom, noting Walker's 1983 definition of womanism and love as an investment in difference: '[L]ove is central to the very definition of the womanist subject who feels love for other women, for humanity, for the spiritual world, for celebration, and, most important, for herself' (Nash, 2011, p. 5). Vital to this self-love is a concern to inhabit and work with the positivity of difference. As Audre Lorde puts it, 'the future of our earth may depend upon the ability of all women to identify and develop new definitions of power and new patterns of relating across difference' (Lorde, 1984, p. 123). As Nash explains, this approach is radical in its 'investment in love as self-worth' (Nash, 2011, p. 12). When love starts as a practice of self-worth it can form the basis for different political communities in the future – a worldmaking utopia built on an ethics of care and held together, not by sameness, but by communal affect and a shared vision.

I recognise that, as a white woman, Emma's practice and conception of love is built on different and particular foundations. And I am mindful that, as Sara Ahmed cautions, acting 'out of love' can shut people out at the same time as it performs an act of openness (Ahmed, 2003). However, I suggest that, in her ideology and practice, Emma's work is infused with the ethics of Black feminist love politics. Considerations of love work *beside* feeling and feminisms, weaving their way throughout the sections that follow. In Section 6, I contextualise Emma's work as love activism, offering an emergent strategy for theatre at this cultural moment.

2 Feminist Underpinnings: Beside Thinking

Are you going to see Wuthering Heights?
Wuthering Heights? That's Kneehigh isn't it?
No it's Wise Children.
Yes, but that's Emma Rice isn't it? . . . It's the same thing. Not really my taste.

The inferences of my exchange with a university colleague got me thinking about the way that Emma's work is positioned or culturally branded.[5] What does this say about mechanisms of control in the industry and in the academy? The work presents conundrums: its populism, patchwork aesthetic, irreverent approach to adaptation, unabashed emotionalism, determinedly utopian hopefulness. But, when we see these aspects as fertile and productive, fuelled with an affirmative politics, we make space to acknowledge its radical potential.

In this section, I overview Emma's career in relation to three binaries allied with her practice: individual/group, text/performance and radical/popular. Working with Eve Sedgewick's 'beside thinking' helps to reconfigure these tensions to move beyond an *either/or* position to *and/with* ways of thinking that redistribute and re-imagine power (Sedgwick, 2003, p. 8). When we consider Emma's trajectory from a gendered perspective, contextualising key influences and critical incidents, its inherent feminism reveals itself. Framing her story in this way reminds us of the *besideness* of the personal and political.

2.1 Individual *and* Group

By creating a company, you are clearly stating that you are no longer an individual. You are opening your arms and shouting 'Come in! I want and need you by my side' I need others to make the work greater than the sum of its parts. But this invitation doesn't mean there are no conditions and it doesn't mean there's no hierarchy. There are both. What it does mean is that the company is bigger than one person. As a leader you've got nowhere to go if you say 'What I say goes'. What happens when you make a mistake? What happens when you want to change your mind? Yes, when everything is going well it would be an ego boost if my company was called 'Emma Rice's Company' but life and work don't always go well. It takes humility and generosity to understand and embrace that.

(Rice, 2022)

Emma's positioning in the UK theatre landscape is inextricably entwined in the tension between the individual and the group. By this I mean the ways in which she manages and builds an ensemble/company and how her individual agency

---

[5] When I use the term 'brand' I am oriented towards cultural branding in terms of class communities, as opposed to commercialisation. Catherine Trenchfield offers a fascinating account of the globalised and commercial branding of Kneehigh in *The Global and Local Appeal of Kneehigh Theatre Company* (Cambridge Scholars: 2022).

as an artist is positioned in relation to that. It feels important to give space to this as I frame Emma's work as a democratic project that strives to redefine humanism, where individualism, as symptomatic of advanced capitalism, is re-imagined (Braidotti, 2022). Returning to the opening exchange, and reiterated in her comment, her identity and (to an extent) agency as an artist is conflated with the group's. Research has shown how women are less likely to 'brand' their practice than men, which, I suggest, underpins a feminist position orientated to collaboration (Peck, 2021, p. 134).

Throughout her career Emma has been committed to working with companies. She was born in 1967 in Chipping Norton, Oxfordshire. Her father, a personnel lecturer, and her mother, a social worker, took her to theatre from an early age. In the 1980s, following an underwhelming experience at secondary school, she completed a BTEC Theatre course at Claringdon Further Education College in Nottingham, led by her lifelong mentor Marielaine Church. BTEC courses (vocational alternatives to A Levels) were first launched in the 1980s, enabling students who sought a less academic and more practical, skills-based education.[6] One could surmise that Emma's sense of herself as anti-intellectual is rooted in this formative education. The experience at Claringdon was foundational for her ideology, process and aesthetics of theatre-making. From a drama hut on the edge of the campus, the student group made a different performance each week, swapping production roles – text, acting, sound, lighting, directing, design.

This multi-disciplined ensemble practice reflected the flattened hierarchy of the women's theatre groups at the time. In the 1980s, identity politics exploded under a Thatcherite government, and whilst the feminist cause, which at the time was built on the common interests of women, was floundering, groups competed for funding (Aston, 2020, p. 4). Feminist scholarship, such as Michelene Wandor's *Carry on Understudies* (1986), pointed to the inequalities for women in British theatre. Women-only theatre companies (Siren, The Woman's Theatre Group, Clean Break) were challenging the male-constructed hierarchies of theatre-making as collectives, with non-hierarchical, democratic ensemble structures (Wandor,1986).

This way of making theatre was not reflected in the traditional conservatoire actor training Emma experienced at Guildhall School of Music and Drama in London where she trained as an actor. In the 1980s and 1990s, drama schools had yet to be affiliated with universities and so followed narrow curriculums where female students were comparatively disadvantaged in a number of ways: there were less places offered to them and their training was stymied by a dearth

---

[6] At sixteen/seventeen years old, UK students choosing to remain in full-time education take A Levels (Advanced Level Qualifications), or more vocational BTECs (Business and Technology Education Council). These courses last for two years.

of challenging female roles, in a naturalistic canon written mostly by dead white males and directed predominantly by male directors. Whilst Emma recalls how one teacher, Sue Lefton, recognised her potential movement ability, she left drama school with a narrow skillset, prepared for an industry where women were outnumbered 2:1 in almost every discipline and misogyny was rife (Peck, 2021 p. 164).

Her first significant job as an actor was with Theatre Alibi, a Theatre-in-Education company started by Exeter drama graduates Tim Spicer and Alison Hodge, which took her back to the multi-disciplined ensemble storytelling and its politics that she had enjoyed at Claringdon. Alibi, in particular Nikki Svedd, who went on to become artistic director, introduced Emma to new complexity in acting/performing – to break the fourth wall, make eye contact and bring the audience into the illusion of the theatrical transformation (Rice, 2022a). This non-naturalistic approach and *communitas* with young audiences was a primal shift in her process. Alibi opened Emma's awareness to European theatre practices, looking beyond Stanislavki and taking her to Poland.

In the 1990s, the work of Polish company Gardzienice impacted a number of UK women practitioners, including director Katie Mitchell, who, as an escape from traditionalism, were drawn to the ideology, aesthetic and raw emotional intensity of their multidisciplinary practice. In 1990, Hodge, who had worked with artistic director Wlodimir Stanievski, secured a grant for Alibi to train in Poland for a month. Stanievski spotted Emma's aptitude and connection to the practice, and she was invited to return as a performer. She spent five transforma-tive months in Poland and the disciplined regime (intensive forty-eight hour physical and vocal training, including night running) changed her body and voice (Rice, 2022a). The ideological shift she experienced was equally trans-formative. Unable to understand the language, she was in a state of high alert, adjusting to the 'no beauty without pain' approach, increasingly aware of the political cost of making theatre. As Poland navigated the transition from communism to a democratic government, political unrest meant that artists were essentially in refuge, in service to their art. The life of a company who lived together, trained together, made theatre together, brought Emma to realise 'this *has* to matter or you don't do it' (Rice, 2022a).

Returning home to her family for Christmas in 1991, Emma chose not to return to the disorientating, authoritarian training regime and throughout the 1990s was thrust into the extremes of the gendered politics in UK theatre and society at large. In the latter part of this decade the New Labour government, with its centrist position, dismantled and de-radicalised the Left. Feminism was fragmented, without a common interest, falling victim to a strategic 'post'-imperative, which suggested that equality had been achieved (Aston,

2020, p. 4). The feminist scholarship, that had started in the 1980s (Case, 1988; Dolan, 1988), gained a groundswell in the 1990s (Phelan, 1993; Grosz, 1994; Aston, 1995; Diamond, 1997; Solga, 2016, pp. 16–17). Whilst female directors and writers started to attract more attention in the media during this decade, the stubborn 2:1 gender disparity within the industry remained.

Connected through their shared experience of Gardzienice, Emma worked with feminist director Katie Mitchell, first as an actor and later as a movement director. Whilst this collaboration was inspirational, introducing her to lifelong friend and colleague, designer Vicki Mortimer, she became frustrated with the roles she was being offered, seeking more creative agency. She briefly fulfilled a long-held dream of working at The National Theatre, when she was cast in an all-female production *Square Rounds* (1992), written and directed by Tony Harrison.[7] However, the politics of the rehearsal room, with its director-led hierarchy and sexism, caused her to quit. She recalls being made to feel like 'a silly little girl who was ruining her career' (Rice, 2022a). Having tasted institutional misogyny, she felt like an outsider in the traditional UK theatre landscape.

When she travelled to Cornwall to audition for Kneehigh in 1994, she found an echo of the Claringdon ethos and the flattened hierarchy of the women's theatre companies. Kneehigh were located in the heart of the countryside, working from a number of barns, in fields near a cliff outside of Gorran Haven. Like Gardzienice, Kneehigh had charismatic male leadership but, unlike Stanievski, Mike Shepherd and Bill Mitchell led with playful anarchy and generosity. On the walls of one of the barns their motto/creed/ mission statement reads: 'generosity, wonder, joy, naughtiness, irreverence, anarchy' (Costa, 2015). They had started as a TIE company, with a focus on story, humour, music, direct address, improvisation, audience interaction, with a punk attitude and DIY aesthetic, producing a type of poor theatre. Their original remit was to serve and develop the Cornish cultural identity. The company welcomed Emma, recognising that she could bring the discipline and ensemble focus of Gardzienice training and, in return, they could help her to find her play, her irreverence and to trust her instincts. She reflects, 'Instead of working with pain to create something beautiful at Kneehigh there was laughter. This was my happy Poland. I found the wild and found the joy' (Rice, 2022a). She joined the company at a time when they had been close to closure due to lack of funding and financial revenue. Her input and impact would be vital in turning their fortunes. She remained with Kneehigh until 2016 when she joined The Globe,

---

[7] National Theatre Archive: https://catalogue.nationaltheatre.org.uk/CalmView/Record.aspx?src=CalmView.Performance&id=1255

as the first female artistic director. As we will see in Section 2.3, moving from company politics and ideology into an institutional structure proved to be particularly challenging.

Wise Children, Emma's current company, started in 2018 with National Portfolio Funding (NPO). It took its name from the Angela Carter novel, their inaugural production at The Old Vic (2018). After *Nights at the Circus* (2005), this was her second adaption/direction of a Carter novel. Kate Kellaway, citing Suzanna Clap, states that a Carter work directed by Rice is 'Plumb in the middle of the feminist project. Neither is the least doctrinaire, both are full of juicy independence' (Kellaway, 2018b). The NPO funding caused controversy as some felt that there was nepotism involved as the company had no track record. This prompted her, for transparency, to share the funding bid online (Kellaway, 2018a). The Arts Council had, effectively, championed Emma and her named collaborators, including the artists she had worked with at Kneehigh (Simon Baker as technical director, Ian Ross and Stu Barker as musical directors and Etta Murfitt as movement director). Lyn Gardner described the formation of Wise Children as 'in effect, the creation of a new family' (Gardner, 2021). Their touring aspirations were stifled by the Covid-19 pandemic but, undaunted, Emma continued to work on building the company's remit, establishing a training arm – Emma Rice's School for Wise Children, developing digital content and mounting three live shows to rave reviews during intermittent lockdowns (*Wise Children*, 2018, *Bagdad Café*, 2019, *Mallory Towers*, 2021). Having relocated from Bristol to Summerset in 2022, Emma's latest move is to buy an old church in the market town of Frome, The Lucky Chance, which will become the local home for Wise Children; somewhere to return to, develop work, store sets and build local networks. For the first time, Emma has sole charge of her destiny – what she makes, where and how she works and with whom.

Overviewing her career, it's interesting to note how being in a company has impacted Emma's autonomy as an artist. Her early contribution to Kneehigh's body of work was subsumed within 'brand Kneehigh' (Trenchfield, 2022). Perhaps her independent agency at The Globe was subsumed by 'brand Globe' or, on the other hand, maybe tensions arose when 'brand Emma' sought autonomy and two cultural entities collided. With Wise Children she has been able to position herself *beside* her company. That said, when looking at the wording of recent reviews, Emma is singled out as the adaptor/director. Despite her reservations, the 'Emma Rice production' is already a cultural brand. However, Emma's steadfast commitment to the ecology of a company – the superior power of the collective imagination, sharing and supporting each other through successes and failures – is a feminist position that, nodding to Braidotti, seeks a new ecology for humanism (Braidotti, 2022).

2.2 Text *and* Performance

> I didn't call my work feminist at the time. Perhaps I didn't have the confidence or perhaps I didn't understand it yet. With hindsight however, I think my work was profoundly feminist. I was looking through a female lens, and storytelling with a female language. I was choosing stories with complex female characters, bubbling with undertones of freedom, expression, empowerment and damage. I was insistent that women's complexity was expressed and explored. A lot of the work was about how women are forced to conform, compelled to survive and strong enough to endure. These stories were not told very often. (Rice, 2022b)

Emma's feminism has evolved and become more explicitly directed as her career has progressed. She started directing in the 2000s, at a time of promise and potential with Tony Blair's New Labour government. Feminist scholarship was starting to turn to new materialisms, to foreground the body and affect (Braidotti, 2002; Haraway, 2003; Sedgwick, 2003). The media suggested that the equality gap in theatre was finally closing, pointing to the rise of female playwrights.[8] In 2005, Helen Edmundson's play *Coram Boy* was the first play by a woman to be performed on the Olivier Stage at The National Theatre, and in 2006 Jude Kelly was the first female artistic director at the Southbank Centre. However, a report on gender in theatre, commissioned for the *Guardian* in 2012, confirmed that the stubborn 2:1 male to female imbalance remained (Peck, 2021, p. 163).

For Emma, this was an extraordinary period of creativity, collaboration and her own personal love affairs. When she directed *The Red Shoes* in 2002, only her second foray in directing, which earned her the Barclays TMA award for Best Director, Emma was going through a divorce from Don Jamieson, who she had worked with at Alibi (see Figure 1). At Kneehigh, she became Mike Shepherd's partner professionally, as artistic director, and romantically (see Figure 2). This is significant because the stories she is drawn to are imbricated in her personal journey at the time, her oeuvre responding to life-changing experiences. This was a decade of love stories – 'bad girl' stories and 'revelation tales' (Rice, 2022b) – where the moral compass spins out of control in the face of passion and heartbreak. After they split in 2008, Emma continued to work in partnership with Shepherd to build 'brand Kneehigh', launching a new mobile theatre structure, The Asylum, growing audiences through ambitious and successful collaborations with The National Theatre, RSC, Bristol Old Vic, Lyric

---

[8] Lauren Bell: *Women in Theatre: The Movers and Shakers*. www.atgtickets.com/blog/women-in-theatre/ (accessed 7 August 2014).

Figure 2 Mike Shepherd and Emma Rice (Kneehigh Barns, Gorran Haven, 2005)

Photo courtesy of Steve Tanner

Hammersmith, Gielgud Theatre and others, and touring, across the United Kingdom and globally. During this period (2001–10), Emma made what was arguably the most successful trilogy in the Kneehigh repertoire, which continued to tour through the next decade – *The Red Shoes* (2001–2, 2010–11), *Tristan and Yseult* (2006, 2013–15) and *Brief Encounter* (2009–10, 2013–14) touring the United Kingdom, the United States and Australia. Kneehigh had multiple shows on at any time, with Emma averaging at least two a year. Her particular theatre language started to find its distinct signature. Critic Lyn

Gardner notes the way that 'An Emma Rice production values clowning as much as it sets store by fine acting; it is likely to meld popular music with classical sounds; and it constantly performs a high-wire act as it negotiates the tragic and the pantomimic, daft comedy and bruising truths' (Gardner, 2021). Pointing to the love activism that drives this Element, she concludes, 'If much British theatre of the last 20 years has been knowing and ironic, Rice's work has been distinctive for the way it wears its heart on its giddy sleeve' (Gardner, 2021).

Notably, reviews from male critics show a pattern of being less effusive. This came to a head in 2007 when the then artistic director of The National Theatre, Nicolas Hytner, called 'dead white male' critics to account for their misogynistic biases, after a string of bad reviews for *A Matter of Life and Death* (Hoyle, 2007). A common feature in male critics' reviews is ambivalence or antagonism towards her adaptations, which one can read as admonishment that a female auteur should have the audacity to mess with canonical texts (Billington, 2009). This sexist critique is rooted in a bias easily attributed to Emma's work – the hierarchy of text over performance (by which I mean non-verbal stagecraft), where text-based theatre is seen to be more 'profitable' in terms of moral and intellectual value (Hurley, 2010, p. 58). This reaffirms Luce Irigaray's 'Law of the Father', privileging the word (reason – male) over the language of the body (emotion – female) (Irigaray, 1985).[9] Perhaps Emma has partly ingested this binary. In interviews she admits a lack of confidence around words, possibly part of her anti-intellectualism and/or a response to the sub-text of reviews. However, her early avoidance of text, where she would 'look for any other way to tell the story' and 'sprinkle the words on top of the action', has shifted in the last decade as the material she works with has become more text heavy (Rice, 2015). From my perspective, Emma's feminist practice inherently blurs the boundaries between theatrical materials, dismantling such dated hierarchies.

Duška Radosavljević considers the labour of theatre-making processes to better understand the constructs, relationship and hierarchies, between text and performance. Her reminder of the original sixteenth- and seventeenth-century company structures, where actor/writers (Shakespeare included) would lead a company, is compelling when thinking about Emma's position as actor/ director/writer. In the nineteenth century, new professions – director, playwright and critic – emerged and compounded the split between text and performance as the theatre critic leaned towards the dominance of text. In much contemporary

---

[9] Luce Irigaray and Hélène Cixous are feminist theorists whose work (along with that of Julia Kristeva) dominates French feminism. This school of feminism is built upon the idea of woman as 'other' than man. Among her many projects, Irigaray invited women to re-claim their power through the sexual pleasures of the body.

theatre practice this remains the case. Radosavljević, citing Jeffrey Richards, considers the split between the writer's 'intellectual theatre' and the 'actor/ actor-manager's widely popular 'theatre of feelings and emotions, theatre of performance and dramatic devices, a Romantic theatre' (qtd in Radosavljević, 2013a, p. 7). This orientation, reflected in Emma's approach, perpetuates the anti-intellectual prejudice towards acting.

Emma maintains her commitment to the story. Storytelling traditions pass down universal tales that teach something of humanity, where, in Brechtian terms, the dialectics, or moments of choice, ask the audience to reconsider their own sense of morality and responsibility for others. Story is at the heart of the ensemble theatre-making of TIE, formative in Emma's early practice. Her body of work retells stories from fairy tales, myths, novels and films, but her choice of story starts with her own personal and emotional connection to the material, 'an itch', that speaks to her at a particular moment (Rice, 2015). Similarly, her adaptation process is led by her own memory of the story (Radosavljević, 2013a). Working from this deeply personal place recalls Hélène Cixous' call for women to write from a deeply personal place of connection, with what she terms as 'écriture feminine' (1976).[10] Emma's feminist theatre-making practice works from and with personal emotion and memory, to tell stories that foreground the female experience, working with the ensemble to discover *why* this story needs to be told, *who* should tell it and *how*.

In this practice there is a flattened hierarchy in terms of theatrical forms. One of the reasons she chooses to work with multi-disciplined artists is to have the largest palette of possibilities when giving shape, texture and resonance to realising the story. As she either authors or co-authors the text, she is able to harness the 'collective imagination' and allow the story to emerge (Rice, 2022b). Text is no more or less important than the actor's movement, voice, lighting, sound and scenography. This reflects the many ways that theatre-making has changed; starting with the twentieth-century split between text-based theatre and the avant-garde, compounded in the 1960s with a move towards audience immersion, then moving to ensemble theatre and devising, pioneered by women's theatre-making in the 1980s. Radosavljević points to the ways in which 'the ensemble way of working itself has challenged and altered the previously held hierarchies of text over performance in the Anglo-American theatre context' (Radosavljević, 2013, p. 23). Perhaps part of the problem is the use of the term 'devising', which is more associated with non-text-based

---

[10] Cixous' theorisation has proved attractive to feminist theatre critics; see Elaine Aston, *An Introduction to Feminism and Theatre* (Routledge, London, 1995) pp. 45–9.

practice. However, I would argue that even when starting with a script there is a form of devising happening.

Whether working with an ensemble of six to devise a fairy tale, a few pages long, or a company of sixteen on a Shakespeare text or adaptation of an epic novel, Emma's process is anti-literary. She never starts from sitting, reading, textual analysis and research – an interrogation of words – she always starts from a place of play, connection and relation to the story, song, movement compositions and scenography. This is deeply embedded in her methodology. Yes, Emma has brought the script to the table from the start, but this remains a spiralling process of discovery, where artists will discover and re-imagine its shape, its edits, its order. In this context, the text/performance binary seems limiting and historical. A hang over from patriarchal practice, which privileges the word and maintains elitist systems and attitudes. Emma's feminist practice, which refuses to privilege the word over action, dissolves such reductive hierarchies.

2.3 Radical *and* Popular

It was so amazing to achieve power in my late forties. It was thrilling to be able to say, This is what I'm going to do and then to actually do it! I have been told so many times that things are not possible and that change has to happen slowly and it's just untrue. We achieved so much in a short time [at The Globe] and I will forever be proud. However, I now believe this speed was why they brought me down. I created change too fast and I didn't bring people with me. That was my mistake. It was a horrible lesson to learn; that meaningful change is possible, it's just that some people don't want it.

I realise as I speak that I am accepting responsibility where perhaps a man wouldn't. I have to remind myself that I brought the administrative team with me, I brought the artists and creative teams with me, I brought the critics with me and, most importantly, I brought the audiences with me. It was a small few with power that couldn't or wouldn't make the leap. I have to remember that, even on bad days.

(Rice, 2022b)

Emma's experience at The Globe saw the dichotomies of traditional/radical and popular/elitist clash in an explosion of conflicting values. Can her work be perceived as both popular *and* radical? In what ways does gender perform in this?

Jason Price, in his study *Modern Popular Theatre*, notes the slipperiness of the term 'popular', for which the Oxford English Dictionary offers dozens of definitions, including reference to 'culturally unrefined' taste and its inter-changeability with folk culture or mass culture (Price, 2016, p. 1). Price posits popular theatre as 'generically defined as theatre by and for the people', where one must necessarily determine *who* those people are at any particular point.

Kneehigh and Emma's 'people' are multi-disciplined and increasingly diverse ensembles, targeting broadly intergenerational audiences, multi-classed, multi-cultural, multifaithed and multi-ethnic. Her early work with Kneehigh was universal in its localism. By targeting a local Cornish audience, the work simultaneously spoke to regional *and* international audiences.

Elsewhere, seeking a definition for popular theatre, Aston and Geraldine Harris turn to John McGrath's 'working-class entertainment' in *A Good Night Out*, pointing to 'directness, comedy, music, emotion, variety, effect, immediacy, and localism (in the sense of both local feel and audience performer relations)' (2015, p. 13). These qualities are present in Emma's work, underpinned with a poetic and feminist sensibility. It is popular in that it is mainstream commercial theatre which, as my opening exchange indicates, provokes conscious or unconscious bias.

Furthermore, given their primary concern with '*A Good Night Out for the Girls*', Aston and Harris review the politicising possibilities of popular feminisms in theatre to dismantle the binaries that see radical social change as antithetical or separate from our need for pleasure and emotional release. They argue that certain hierarchies of thinking maintain elitist cultural systems and knowledge production: mind over body, reason over emotion, intellect over experience, rational over instinct, culture over nature, cynicism over positivity, negativity over affirmation, male over female (and I would add), text over performance and individual over group (Aston and Harris, 2015). Harnessing critical feminisms, they dismantle these structures to re-orientate the popular *as* radical, working with affect and the reparative as antidotes to the paranoid imperative and the discursive turn. Erin Hurley's work on theatre and feeling, which suggests that theatre *either* aspires to profit (in terms of educative and political social profit) *or* pleasure (in terms of simple enjoyment), offers a provocation to popular feminisms, which loosen these boundaries, enabling both affects to happen *beside* each other (Aston and Harris, p. 24). This speaks to Jill Dolan's call for a reparative, utopian theatre, reaching across difference, for a renewed sense of humanity through empathy and solidarity (Dolan, 2005).

Working from the affirmative underpins Emma's approach; that this might be seen to be simplistic or naive is troubling. She is determined to avoid 'any cynicism' (some might read intellectualism) 'coming between the audience and the story' (Rice, 2015). She maintained the same commitment to accessibility when she moved to The Globe: 'The biggest crime is if anyone comes out of The Globe saying, "That was boring" or, "I didn't understand it". Then we have failed' (Gardner, 2016a). If such inclusivity does not appeal to academic taste or, in the case of The Globe, upsets cultural purists, then one must ask who and what theatre is for? Equally troubling is the idea that emotionally driven storytelling somehow dumbs down political affect. Aston and Harris contest this idea as they resituate sentimentality and emotion, easily dismissed as vacuous, indulgent and passive, as mobilising and agitating materials (2015, pp. 15–16). Similarly, in its affecting capacity and impressive touring impact, Emma's work has the potential to 'move' large numbers of people across the world to feel/see/think again about what it is to be human, thus activating the radical (by which I mean politically transformative) *beside* the popular. In this regard, Duška Radoslavljević perhaps offers the most fitting elucidation when, writing about Kneehigh, she refers to their practice as 'subversive populism' as opposed to 'explicit radicalism' (Radosavljević, 2015, p. 156). She argues that through appealing to audiences with commercially successful adaptations which are then re-authored, the work becomes a 'continuous political act that has provoked and challenged some established models of theatre-making' (Radosavljević, 2015, p. 158).

When we dismiss the popular as being anti-intellectual, simplistic, indulgent and naïvely optimistic, we perpetuate value systems that negate change. What does this say about those who are *not* open to this type of work? These biases reaffirm the mechanisms of control and cultural branding that positions of privilege maintain in order to protect their own value systems. Who gets to decide what is radical? What is worthy of scholarship? When the theatre industry is having to constantly redefine itself, surely popular work, that has the potential to bring people together, to affect bodies, to shift our ways of seeing, is vital.

For Emma, whose gendered and classed identity has been publicly called to account, questions of unconscious bias have followed her career. She notes that 'There are gatekeepers of theatre in this country. I have never fitted in, so I see them clearly. Most of the gatekeepers went to Oxbridge and read classics and have similar taste in theatre' (Rice, qtd in Kellaway, 2018). Identity politics has come to define the twenty-first century.[11] The feminist revival prompted by the *#Me Too* movement in 2017[12] and the outpouring of fury about ongoing sexual violence against women in 2021, after the death of Sarah Everard, raped and murdered by serving Met officer Wayne Couzins, has seen a shift towards

---

[11] The death of George Floyd by a white policeman in 2020 which caused a global uprising for Black Lives Matter, prompting recognition of institutional racism with wide-scale calling-out across industries, including in UK theatre and in drama schools. There was a wave of resignations and new appointments, a notable shift towards female principals and initiatives to decolonise the curriculum in all educational sectors.

[12] The *#Me Too* movement, started by Alyssa Milano in 2006, a global campaign to speak out about sexual violence, which garnered attention in 2017, was prompted by public accusations from many high-profile female actors of sexual harassment and assault by Harvey Weinstein, an influential US film producer.

a revival of feminisms, akin to the feminist energies of the second wave, where a new generation come together to recover and radicalise democracy (Aston, 2020, p. 3). Campaigns for gender equality and diversity change in theatre have gained traction, including Tonic Theatre, founded by Lucy Kerbel in 2011, and The Act for Change project in 2014. Scholarship has sought to re-orientate and offer strategies. Feminist scholars (Braidotti, 2011; Haraway, 2016; Bennet, 2010), pointing to posthuman feminism, bringing together ecofeminists, technofeminists and new materialists, look to restorative systems and new ways of living together in the world, recognising the need to rethink what being a human being means in the 'new normal'. In theatre, there has been a wave of female artistic director appointments: Josie Rourke at the Donmar (2012–19); Indhu Rubasingham at Tricycle Theatre (2012); Erica Whyman as Deputy and then Acting Artistic Director of the RSC (2013); and, in 2016, Emma Rice at The Globe.[13]

Emma's tenure at The Globe foregrounded questions of identity politics. In 2016, when she left Kneehigh to take up the prestigious position as its first female artistic director, she met a number of challenges: for the first time she was running a building as opposed to a company; she was tied to one place as opposed to touring; she was programming across seasons and stages, working simultaneously with multiple teams; she had only ever directed one Shakespeare play with Kneehigh (*Cymbeline*, 2007/8) to mixed reviews; she had freely shared her difficulty and resistance to working with the language of Shakespeare; and she was working with a board of trustees outside of her choice who were not creatives. During her period at The Globe (2016–18), Emma made four new works (*A Midsummer Night's Dream* and *Twelfth Night* for the main stage, *Little Match Girl* and *Romantics Anonymous* for Wanamaker) and programmed thirty-two. Her two seasons, *The Wonder Season* and *The Summer of Love*, broke box office records and received largely positive reviews. However, some critics were poised for attack, questioning the inclusion of amplified sound and electric lighting in a building whose very purpose was historical authenticity. Richard Morrison's headline read, 'The Globe has been a success story. Why is Emma Rice wrecking it?' (Morrison, 2016). During her brief tenure she was a trailblazer: the first UK artistic director to pledge fifty–fifty gender parity and 40 per cent Black and global majority employment; pushing the boundaries of staging Shakespeare in ways that, to my thinking, drew attention to elitist attitudes and cultural snobbery. However, the pace of such progress was too radical for some and, in 2017, after a period of disagreement between her and the board, who were concerned that her use of stage

---

[13] Despite the wave of female appointments to buildings, 63 per cent of the directors of (NPO's), receiving longer-term funding from the Arts Council, continue to be male (Aston, 2020, p. 4).

lighting and amplified sound was running contrary to The Globe's remit for historically 'authentic' staging, it was announced that her tenure would end (Furness, 2017). This provoked outcry about The Globe being essentially a heritage site rather than a theatre, about gender, class and the cultural elite (Gardner, 2016b).

In the Wise Children Summer School, Emma wore a T-shirt with 'Radical' emblazoned on the front (2022).[14] One can't deny that the changes she initiated at The Globe were radical. Her reflection at the start of this section cuts to the complexity of gender, class and power as inscribed and inscribing. How her cultural brand of popular *and* radical might have affected inclusivity had her tenure continued will remain unknown. My sense is that the popular needs to be reconceived for its radical potential if we are to push against walls and dissolve boundaries. Whilst the same gatekeepers, taste makers and knowledge producers set the agenda and brand culture, nothing will change.[15] Contrastingly, Feminist *thinking beside* makes space for the in-between and the generative. Audre Lorde puts it this way: 'The future of our earth may depend on the ability of all women to identify new definitions of power and new patterns of relating across difference' (Lorde, 2017, p. 105). Surveying Emma's career – her evolving feminist body of work, its form and content, ethics and principles – points to theatre-making unabashed in its utopic purpose, striving for a more hopeful way of being together in the world, underpinned by feminisms.

3 Affecting Practice: Ethics of Affirmation

assemblage:

1 a collection of persons or things: gathering – [*who*]
2 the act of assembling: the state of being assembled – [*how*]
3 a. an artistic composition made from scraps, junk and odds and ends – [*what*]
    b. the art of making assemblages [*how*][16]

A consideration of *assemblage* as a theatre-making process and practice is compelling when seeking apposite definition for Emma's work. It conjures its

---

[14] The Wise Children Summer School ran from 25th to 29th July in Oxford.

[15] It is important to note that since 2018, there has been ongoing progressive work around representation and identity at the Globe in its policies, programming and education provision, including the yearly Shakespeare and Race festival led by Professor Farah Karim- Cooper, the anti-racist programme of events https://www.theguardian.com/stage/2022/oct/27/shakespeare-black-racist-festival-race-globe and the production of *I, Joan* (2022), with Joan of Arc depicted as non-binary, https://www.standard.co.uk/culture/theatre/i-joan-shakespeares-globe-review-non-binary-game-changer-women-b1022607.html. These initiatives have seen subsequent hate-speech from opponents of such work on social media, as well as reactionary coverage in the right-wing media.

[16] Miriam-Webster Dictionary definition. I have added the words in brackets to indicate how I am using this term in different ways in relation to Emma's work.

shape, qualities, texture and affect in ways that alternatives, such as total theatre, fail to do. But how can scholarship hope to capture the shared process of an ensemble, its fluid, transversal movement, its felt sense? As a researcher I draw on fieldwork spanning seven years, including observations of rehearsal for *Tristan and Yseult*, (2013–14) and *Rebecca* (2015), research and development for *Blue Beard* (2022) and *The Buddha of Suburbia* (2022), the Wise Children Summer School (2022) and interviews with Emma and collaborators.

As the dictionary definition attests, assemblage has various meanings, the *who*, *what* and *how* of which [my additions] orientate and shape my analysis. I've been drawn to the political potential of *assemblage* through the work of Simon Bowes, which attends to the situated political affect of the assembly and to assemblage in Fine Art, combining various objects into an integrated whole. Bowes argues for a 'deeper reflexive awareness of assemblage as a concept and a material practice' as 'an aesthetics, a politics, an ecology of embodiment and desire' (Bowes, 2019, p. 29). He has been influenced by Gilles Deleuze and Félix Guattari's view of assemblage as 'constellations of singularities' (Deleuze and Guattari, 1987, p. 406), and as multiplicities 'constituted by heterogeneous terms' which establish 'relations between them' (Deleuze and Parnet 2007, p. 52). These singularities maintain specificity without collapsing into oneness, reminding us of Hannah Arendt's call for productive social movements, where individuals maintain uniqueness within the group's plurality (Arendt,1998). In relation to Emma's work, I note this quality as a feature of her ensemble practice. As critic, Dominic Cavendish, writing about Kneehigh, suggests, 'few companies combine such ensemble zest with such individual truth' (Cavendish, 2006).

Rosi Braidotti refers to 'heterogenous assemblages' as fundamental to her posthuman feminist project for human–non-human interconnectedness where '"We"-who-are-not-one-and-the-same-but-are-in-*this*-together' (Braidotti, 2022, p.8). Emma's theatre, through its ontological relationality, works with the capacity for people to affect and be affected in mutual interdependence. This happens *between* people (creative team, performers and audience) and *with* objects – instruments, puppets, props, costumes, text – which, collectively, creates affect. Braidotti describes the practice of making affective connections across domains as 'transversal' and 'spiritual', working with an 'ethics of affirmation as political praxis', where 'desire, freedom and becoming' are shared collectively by kindred spirits (Braidotti, 2022, pp. 102–4). If we follow this line of thinking, Emma's practice as assemblage produces moral value, promoting love and hope. The 'transversal' political praxis comes to matter through *who* she works with, the alternative kinship of her assembly; *what* she works with, the materials themselves and the way of assembling them; and *how* she works, with an ethics of affirmation.

3.1 Alternative Kinship, Temporary Communities

I think I drift in a slightly other world. I often feel on the outskirts. It's hard to describe. I don't fit in London. I don't fit in the industry. I don't quite fit in the centre of things. And that off-centre tilt gives me an instability. It creates oxygen and space around me; a space into which surprising things come.

(Rice, 2022b)

Who are Emma's assembly? At the end of Wise Children Summer School, she advised the group to 'find your people'.[17] Kneehigh have been variously described by critics as misfits, anarchists, madcaps and a motley crew, meaning an unusual mixed group. Emma's perception of her own 'otherness' is essential to her artistic identity. She describes 'her people' as 'left-handed', similarly 'on the outskirts', a motley crew drawn to alternative spaces – a queer kinship (Rice, 2022b). She brings people together for their 'spirit' and 'energy' as much as for their talent. Many in the assembly have worked with Kneehigh for decades and now have director positions in Wise Children, including composers Stu Barker and Ian Ross, choreographer Etta Murffit and sound designer Simon Baker. She continues to work regularly with designer Vicki Mortimer, lighting designer Malcom Rippeth, puppet maker Sarah Wright and photographer Steve Tanner. Previous writing collaborators included Anna Maria Murphy and Carl Grose. Regular performers include Annette McLoughlin, Dot Attkinson, Lizzie Winkler, Katy Owen, Tamzin Griffin, Amanda Lawrence, Beck Appleby, Éva Magyar, Patrycja Kujawska, Nandi Bhebhe, Mike Shepherd, Tristan Sturrock, Craig Johnson, Gareth Snook, Giles King, Dave Mynne and Jim Carey. The Wise Children production team includes Poppy Keeling (executive producer), Steph Curtis (general manager), Helen Comerford (participation producer), Laura Keefe (head of performance) and Rhys Bugler (assistant producer). All are 'singularities in the constellation', offering particular skills, occupying shared space, coming together, unique and plural.

What holds a community together? Arendt points to 'the force of mutual promise or contract' (Arendt,1998, p. 244). As previously noted, on the walls of the Kneehigh barns the creed or contract was written large: 'generosity, wonder, joy, naughtiness, irreverence, anarchy' (Costa, 2015). Wise Children's 2018 Mission Statement outlines their two aims: 'To bring world-class work to audiences across the UK' and 'To train a new and more diverse generation of theatre practitioners'.[18] Mutual promise translates to a familial bond, and Emma repeatedly refers to her 'theatre family' (Rice, 2015, 2022b). This trope spans from the generational commedia dell'arte troupes in the sixteenth century, to the

---

[17] The Summer School ran between 25 and 29 July 2022 in Oxford.
[18] Wise Children Mission Statement shared with author via email with Helen Comerford.

lineages of contemporary British thespian families, fondly parodied by Angela Carter in *Wise Children*. Whether blood-related or not, the familial apostology of theatre companies is a dominant form of knowledge production where a shared language, or shorthand, is handed between members of a company. Mortimer, in conversation with Emma, comments, 'You recognise each other, whether you're working together or not, there's a sense of knowing what your shared DNA is' (Mortimer, 2020). Emma's formative experience with two companies living, working, and in the case of Kneehigh, touring the world together – deepened by life–love–work relationships within the company – inevitably shapes this as her alternative 'family of choice' (Rice, 2020b).

Her approach to nurturing the ensemble has necessarily changed to be more fluid, recognising that these are long-term collaborations and there's a benefit to people leaving and returning (Rice, 2022b). What brings them back is the work and the process – her 'kind rehearsal room' (Owen, 2022), and the multi-disciplined team she brings together to make 'alchemy' (Bhebhe, 2022). Performers move from singing to playing an instrument, from dancing to operating a puppet, from acting to acrobatics – the multiplicity of bodies made manifest. As stated in Section 2, Emma seeks this multi-disciplinarity from her ensemble as it offers the richest potential palette from which to assemble the story. The shared theatre language, crafted over three decades, has evolved into a distinct methodology. Tristan Sturrock, who has worked with Emma since 1990, reflects on how she re-orientated Kneehigh's practice, bringing Polish intensity, truth and discipline, *beside* their clowning and playfulness, maintaining both within tight parameters, clear structure and imaginative vision (Sturrock, 2022). She has continued to nurture this methodology with the demands of new material and collaborators, bringing through young talent with Wise Children, and making a home for the company in Somerset, at the church of Lucky Chance, renovated in 2022.

The audience is another vital 'singularity' within the constellation. From her formative experience of TIE, Emma has stayed true to the power of direct contact with audiences. It is, I would argue, the most vital feature of her aesthetic and essential to its affecting potential. Breaking the fourth wall calls for a shared responsibility – a desire to create *communitas*. This term, popularised by anthropologist Victor Turner, describes moments in theatre where the audience feel themselves to be part of the whole in a way which may feel political and/or spiritual. For Dolan, in her formulation of the utopian performative, it is sharing the 'hopeful feeling of what the world might be like if every moment of our lives were . . . emotionally voluminous, generous, aesthetically striking, and intersubjectively intense' (Dolan, 2005, p. 5). In Emma's work, the fourth wall is broken through staging conceits, for example in *Brief Encounter* (2009) or *Nights in the Circus* (2005), where performers appear from the auditorium; through event, the flicking of the coin by a member of the audience in *Matter of Life and Death* (2007) to decide the outcome of the story; or through large-scale participation, the audience joining performers for a slow dance at the end of *Don John* (2008). Eye contact defines the acting style, with Emma giving her actors notes such as 'Put it out!' (Bhebhe, 2022) and 'Less acting! More storytelling!' (McCormick, 2022). For Katie Owen, a performer widely celebrated for her clowning, direct eye contact is crucial 'When you are looking somebody straight in their eyes, people feel that connection immediately. I'm listening so fully to them. For comedy performers it's the toughest thing and the best thing because you are feeding off that response' (Owen, 2022). The relational production of affect between audience and performers produces what Emma has described as the 'human snowball' of emotion: a *communitas*, where people share a space of uncertainty and vulnerability together (Rice, 2022b). This extends the ripples and reach of alternative kinship, celebrating the positivity of difference. Speaking to Lucy Kerbel from Tonic Theatre, Emma's reflections echo Braidotti's paradigm for posthuman feminism: '"We"-who-are-not-one-and-the-same-but-are-in-*this*-together' (2022, p. 8). She says, 'I call it the temporary community. There's something about the human condition in that we come together in groups and listen to stories that makes us feel that life is manageable; we feel part of a community, we sing songs and look other people in the eye and say, "we're in this together"' (Rice, 2016).

3.2 Assemblage for Affect

> The shows are emotional because of a human domino effect. The chain starts with the truth of my own connection to subject matter. When I choose a story there's an instinctive, irresistible and truthful understanding of the 'why'. My job is to share and explore that connection. First, I share it with my creative team, my actors and musicians. These artists, in turn, share their emotional response and lived experience with me. This snowball of human experience informs every corner of the work until we finally share our story with the audience. And, if we've done our job well, the show will meet the emotional experience of the audience. They become part of this glorious chain: the final domino in the run. It is this connection and this visceral jolt that creates the emotion.
>
> (Rice, 2022b)

As the assembler, Emma gathers, selects and arranges her materials (text, acting, design, sound, lighting, set, props) to organise the story's energy and affective potential. Time – rhythm, pace and resonance – propels the emotional arc of the story to produce affect. I think of this as an orchestration, assembling moods, textures and tones of events through tempo – conducting the exchange of energies between performers and audience. In this section, I first consider her methodology, and then focus on her use of chorus and the way that non-human objects (which I refer to as thing-ness) operate in this practice.

Her process, deciding what materials are needed and how to assemble them, is a methodology honed over three decades. In 2013, in conversation with Duška Radosavljević, Emma explained the stages of a typical five-week rehearsal process: weeks one and two are entering into the story and the play-world, reading the chosen edition or script together, practicing daily physical games and warm ups, building the foundations of the 'why' of the story, producing lists of themes, problem areas and creative responses, including drawings; pre-written musical numbers would be learnt, choreographies explored and characters created collectively; from week two, scenes, musical numbers and choreographies are staged and assembled (Radosavljevic, 2013a, pp. 101–3). Tristan Sturrock notes how Emma's own multi-disciplinarity – coming to directing as a performer and choreographer, with design sensibility from working with Bill Mitchell – gives her a wide palette. She sets tasks from a performer's perspective – ensuring clear parameters to allow for freedom to play, building 'little blocks' or 'islands' of performance to shape and edit and finding the most interesting perspectives from which to tell the story (Sturrock, 2022). In their colour, mood and texture, these 'islands', where acting, dance, music and stagecraft converge, could be seen as phrases of affect, orchestrating the emotional score of the story – layers of snow in the human snowball.

Adding to this overview, Research and Development (R&D), normally three to five days, happens months before rehearsals start. Emma introduces key collaborators to join her in building the imaginative world of the story – to test material, build set numbers, order the events and gather ideas. In the R&D for *Blue Beard* (2022), Emma invited composer Stu Barker, choreographer Etta Murfitt, four performers and her production team, with a visit from designer Vicki Mortimer. She had already met with Barker and shared lyrics for four songs, written two short scenes and gathered a Pinterest assemblage of visual images. Emma's world of the story, why she wants to tell it and from whose perspective, has already partially landed. As noted in Section 2, her own personal connection to the story underpins her feminist practice. The process usually starts with poetry, the lyrics of songs and set pieces that the ensemble learn to play musically, vocally and choreographically. Notably, these songs speak directly to the politics of the work, providing an architecture of ideas from the start. She meets her collaborators in this shared world and they enrich it with their unique spirits, their energies and their impulses which she harvests and assembles. The resonances of the ensemble, their emotional responses and their passions serve the story. When working with a shared language affect phrases are built quickly; in three days a shared visual, aural and emotional world was created with four songs, two scenes, design ideas and one dance. Additionally, in some processes, a puppeteer or circus performer might be brought in to work with the performers and set pieces created. From this compositional score the process operates with clear parameters allowing material to be arranged very quickly.

Moving on to the convention of the chorus, whilst Emma builds ensemble practice, the form, aesthetic, ideology and methodology of chorus is at the heart of her storytelling. The chorus provides the political perspective which, in its turn, shapes the emotional affect. She reflects, 'By knowing who's telling the story, you know which story to tell and why you are doing it' (Rice, 2022b). The Western tradition of choral storytelling has its roots in Greek Theatre and is a feature of Brechtian form, where the illusion of naturalism is punctured through alienation devices: all stagecraft happening in full view and direct address with the audience. This allows for a shared theatrical contract where 'we're going to look at each other, play with each other, and then absolutely go 100 per cent into the truth of it, but be able to step out again' (Rice, 2022b). Knowing who is narrating gives her a particular perspective from which she can write and assemble. Her choruses repeatedly, recalling Gayatri Spivak, give voice to the 'subaltern' (Spivak, 1988). This shifts the position from the traditional Greek chorus, usually, but not always, representing the voice of the polis, to the minoritarian – outsiders, misfits and motley crews. Her chorus in *Red Shoes* (2002) were the cowards in the First World War, nursing hidden shame and trauma. In *Tristan and Yseult* (2006), the Love Spotters, with their cagouls, birdwatching binoculars and balaclavas search for love, again nursing their shame. In the R&D for *Blue Beard* (2022), a chorus of 'fearless, fucked and furious' nuns had escaped a patriarchal system. By giving the storytelling to the outsider, the queer and, in the case of *Wuthering Heights* (2022), the non-human, Emma gives agency to the oppressed position and taps into the affect of shame. This powerfully affecting shared position potentially opens us to compassion and to changing perspectives. Reflecting on the fallibility of the characters in Emma's body of work, Mortimer argues that this asks for 'our agreement, as an audience, to forgive the transgressions, forgive the mistakes, forgive the fuckups and see the mirror. So that by forgiving the characters, and seeing them as faulty, human, we're also able to come away at the end of the performance and feel that forgiveness is somehow in ourselves as well. There's an instinctive compassion in that' (Mortimer, 2020).

When a chorus of storytellers is the foundation of the ensemble, a particular politics is built that enables a shared responsibility. As Nandi Bhebhe reflects, this means 'you are always part of the whole . . . you're not there for yourself, you're there collectively to tell the story' (Bhebhe, 2022). This creates a feeling of support, *communitas* and mutuality. In the process, whilst performers may be tasked with working on separate scenes, they are all brought together to watch each other's work. This sense of witnessing, inherent in the process, is there in the Brechtian-influenced staging, where all remain on stage watching the unfolding action, setting up the stagecraft for scenes, always in attendance to the story and to each other.

Furthermore, it is important to note the affect of comedy. Following Lecoq, many of Emma's choruses are clowns, often wearing unifying costume in place of a red nose. For example, in *Tristan and Yseult* (2006), the chorus of the 'Unloved' wore cagoules with hoods up and surveyed the audience through binoculars. As clowns, this chorus performed their failure and their shame through visual gags, mistakes and mis-timings. They were both plural and unique, maintaining their individuality *and* part of a group. We laughed at them and with them, joining in shared compassion.

In *Wuthering Heights* (2022), the chorus was non-human – the Yorkshire Moor as storyteller. This was closer to a Greek chorus: composer Ian Ross and the group developed a type of sing-speak, as opposed to choral speaking. Ross, who is interested in the pattern of speech in music, shaped this other-worldly form of choral vocalising, giving rhythm and musicality to the text, whilst working with speech patterns. This allowed for individual voices to maintain their unique variation and so created a type of collective voicing. The company worked with the inter-connectiveness of nature, the mycelium, 'the plant life, the birds, the weather' to create the character (Ross, 2022). One of the performers, Nandi Bhebhe, reflects, 'The costume I have has some weight to it, the sense that it's been here for centuries, eons. And it's not just that place [Yorkshire], it's as far out as the earth stretches, it's ancient. So there's something about being dragged through time as well' (Bhebhe, 2022). Here the subaltern is non-human, cellular, molecular and elemental. In this thematic, which can be seen throughout Emma's work, I see Braidotti's posthuman feminism at work (see Figure 3).

And finally, turning to *thing-ness*, Emma's refusal at The Globe to reduce her artistic palette, with the loss of electric lighting and amplified sound, draws attention to the agency of the non-human, or *thing-ness*, in her practice. This echoes Jane Bennet's 'theory of distributive agency', which sees the non-human as actants (Bennet, 2010). The human/non-human arrangements of the assemblage are evident in Emma's rehearsal room which allows for multi-occupancy: an area for the band, a clothes rail with costumes, various bags of props, puppets, craft materials and the requisite production table. This set-up replicates Kneehigh's hallowed Goran Haven Barns, a theatrical playground where creatives build the world of the story together, using everything around them –

Figure 3 Emma Rice in *Women of Troy* (1991) dir. Katie Mitchell
Photo courtesy of Emma Rice

a type of theatre-making club house. The impact of having multi-disciplined artists together in this space creates a particular type of creativity, intensely liberating and transformative, producing a childlike quality of playfulness. Emma laughingly calls it 'after school club' (Rice, 2022); people immerse themselves in imaginative worlds, where an everyday object becomes whatever you dream it to be, a costume produces a different you. The effect of musicians rehearsing, at the same time as choreography is devised, whilst props are being constructed and acting scenes rehearsed, does produce a particular type of alchemy.

Returning to Deleuze and Parnet, the assemblage is conjured from groupings of diverse elements, 'made up of many heterogenous terms', which establishes 'relations between them' (Deleuze and Parnet, 2002, p. 69). Five types of non-human actants in Emma's process can be seen to make up this heterogenous, relational assemblage. These can be categorised as functional – for example the balls used to play warm up games, and the pens and paper used to map ideas; stimuli – the books and artefacts, including music, used to inspire the imagination; theatrical – including texts, costumes and props; and puppets and instruments. On day two of *Blue Beard*, for instance, the ensemble was asked to work on a crafting task in relation to the themes of the story – to perform 'an illusion' using any available objects. They were engrossed in cutting, sticking, colouring, shaping materials and working their artistic and design muscles alongside their musicality and physical expression. Emma jokingly referred to this as 'art club', part of the multimodal assemblage, alongside dance, text and music club (Rice, 2022).

Watching musicians in relation with their instruments or, during the Wise Children summer school, performers working with puppets, a sense of 'distributive agency' is visceral and the affect is palpable. When performers work with puppets, the agency shifts from human to non-human. Operators (there are normally at least two) try to tap into the emotional textures, the breath, the spirit of the object, animating it together, working with deep listening and transferring their energy through the puppet with their gaze, which is always *towards* the puppet. Equally, musicians hold instruments as extensions of their bodies, sounding, resonating and vibrating. The sound produced immediately affects the mood, hitting the emotional sensitivity of the listener. When watching Barker plucking the twanging chords of a hurdy-gurdy, we enter a different world – returning to Erin Hurley – a world of felt sense, of mood (Hurley, 2010). Barker and Ross' signature music is, arguably, the most immediately affecting material in Emma's assemblage. Mortimer, talking with Emma about her choice of music said, 'It's like access to the audience's nerve centres somehow. You have an incredible instinct for what music hits a moment. A piece of music starts and my little fuzzy hairs are standing up, because it's so right for the moment, and the associations are so true' (Mortimer, 2020). Akin to Braidotti's posthuman feminism, these relational connections between human, non-human and audience are transformative – the transversal in action – an affecting assemblage.

3.3 An Ethics of Affirmation

We've all got the fear of not being good enough. You protect yourself until you can say through gritted teeth, 'This is the best I can be'. My process smashes this 'fight' response out of the water. There's no fun in fear. There's no surprise in fighting. I create an environment where nothing is scary. We trust each other enough to say anything, dare to do anything, risk anything. Only in this fear free space can wonder happen.

(Rice, 2022b)

The first time I entered Emma's rehearsal room for *Tristan and Yseult* (2014) I felt the love. I was late and nervous, having come from rehearsal with another director, in whose space I felt obliged to perform invisibility. When I came through the door, everyone in the room, including the production team, was playing what appeared to be a joyfully competitive ball game. Emma stopped the game, introduced me, explained the rules and invited me to join them. We threw ourselves into it – foolishly flopping, encouraging, teasing, boldly holding each other up. The ethics of affirmation in practice comes into being through the affect of pleasure and this speaks loudly to the love and care of ecofeminism's 'heterogenous assemblages' noted at the start of Section 3. What produces pleasure in this process? Why is it that I smile more, laugh more, feel bolder, feel energised?

People literally wear their hearts on their sleeves. There is a familial fashion for T-shirts with motivational texts: in *Blue Beard* (2022), a number of the Wise Children cast wore T-shirts emblazoned with 'What a Joy it is to Dance and Sing'; Etta Murfitt's read 'Believe in Love and Joy'; during the summer school Emma's read 'Radical'. Perhaps, returning to Arendt, a mutual promise or contract is subliminally at work through these mottos, producing a positive mood which helps to calm nerves. Bhebhe remarks on the inevitable fear experienced when joining a new ensemble and how, for her, starting with the text can feel daunting and inhibiting whilst Emma's process, where everyone starts by playing games and learning the same material, songs and choreographies, 'puts everyone in the park together', flattening hierarchies (Bhebhe, 2022). The team games, played every day at the start of rehearsal, are vital in enabling this trust. These draw on familiar playground/sports re-imaginings: volleyball, where every fifth hit has to be a body part; tongue twister memory games where you have to maintain a beat; keepy-uppy ball games with forfeits. They have been honed over years. There is team talk between players, for example 'Double Dibbs!' if the ball is touched twice or 'Wanker Shot!' if played too aggressively. Emma either plays with the team or acts as coach/adjudicator. The games test and sharpen a number of skills: the technical skills of alertness, impulse, balance, precision, spatial awareness, focus, listening, sensing; and the personal and social qualities of teamwork – giving and receiving, generosity, responsibility, trust, boldness, commitment, forgiveness, empathy, compassion. Both sets of knowledges happen *beside* each other. When everyone is relying on each other, there is an immediate and deeply felt human connection.

There is a lot of laughter in the room. Emma's sense of humour, her naughtiness and sense of play is motivating and affirming. Owen reflects, 'the laughter in the rehearsal room translates onto the stage as you can see that the actors have this connection with each other, looking at each other with a spark in their eyes and there's a playfulness that sometimes gets lost in translation between rehearsals and performance' (Owen, 2022). This enables performers to take risks. Emma's feedback 'Strong but wrong!' encapsulates the clowning trope that flopping is only ever a resource (Peck, 2021, p. 183). For Sturrock, this enabling atmosphere is gendered, 'With a female in charge or leading the process you feel that there's a softer edge, that allows you to be more vulnerable, to make a leap into somewhere you'd normally be reticent about, which gives you an even bigger palette'(Sturrock, 2022). In this I see the 'engaged peda-gogy' of bell hooks, where the learning exchange foregrounds the well-being of both teacher/director (in this case Emma) and learners (her collaborators), which aims to foster hope and love. For hooks, whilst the teacher holds the ultimate responsibility, authority is constantly passed between participants, which enables confidence (hooks, 2010).

Emma harnesses the strengths of her collaborators and enables the collective imagination. Her experience as a performer means that she has developed a methodology where tight parameters – everyone has very clear tasks and the vision is shared – allow artists to play from their impulse. As Owen suggests, this shared responsibility, playfulness and bold-hearted spirit is embodied in performance. Mortimer, in conversation with Emma, reflects:

> What your process of bravery achieves is a real sort of lifeline connection between an inception of a project, and what arrives in the live space with the audience. It's the Holy Grail. It's what we're all looking for, is how you make a performance remain live. Even though decisions have necessarily been made and the editorial process has refined and defined the necessary rules for production you absolutely want the life force to be still available. I think that's what your process achieves in a way that I've never really seen with the same prickly neck thing in anybody else's work. (Mortimer, 2020)

Emma's dialogue in rehearsal is insightful when thinking about the politics of this practice. There are repeated phrases that develop the technique/aesthetic that carry her theatre-making wisdom: 'Think-forget-think-forget! Louder is always a good note! Let's make it funnier! Stagecraft – Nothing to see! Musicality! Musicality! Musicality! Repetition is the friend to the actor! Let's mess it up!' And there is the coaching feedback that builds confidence: 'You are all doing awfully well! Do it again, but better! Strong but wrong! Lovely seeing everyone magnificent! You are at the peak of your powers!' (Rice, 2014, 2022)[19]. This language is both authoritative and supportive – undeniably affirming. Her insistence that the work be accessible, 'without any cynicism coming between the performers and the audience', is reflected in her attitude towards critique, which, for her, isn't useful in the creative process when you are trying to 'diffuse doubt, complexity, people putting up barriers and obstacles'. As such, she never criticises her team but doesn't shy away from 'guiding them or even stopping things'. Similarly, she dis-encourages preparation as 'the more you work, the more you cover up what your instinctive understanding is'. For

---

[19] I observed Emma using this coaching dialogue in fieldwork during 2014 rehearsal for *Tristan and Yseult* in London and in 2022 during the Research and Development of *Bluebeard* in Somerset.

Emma, preparation is normally preparing not to fail, not helpful to a practice where 'failure is much more interesting' (Rice, 2022b).

In *Notes toward a Performative Theory of Assembly*, Judith Butler asks us to consider what holds the assemblage together, 'what are their conditions of persistence and of power in relation to their precarity and exposure?' (2015, pp. 73–4). What holds the singularities of Emma's assemblage together might be best understood through what Manuel DeLanda terms symbiosis or 'sympathy' (DeLanda, 2016, p. 2). Might this force of sympathy be a type of love? Love for each other, love for the work, love for the way of working? Could Mortimer's 'holy grail' be the affect of love? Emma suggests, 'In a group [creatives and audience], excitement happens, kindness happens, revelation happens. There is a world where more "What if? What if?" happens' (Rice, 2022b). This captures the essence of Dolan's utopian theatre, enabling 'a more capacious sense of a public, in which social discourse articulates the possible, rather than the insurmountable obstacles to human potential,' where 'expressions of hope and love' allow for 'a more abstracted notion of "community", or for an even more intangible idea of "humankind"' (Dolan, 2005, p. 2). Emma's posthuman assemblage, the ethos of the rehearsal exchange and the *communitas* of performance produce an ethics of affirmation that works from the positivity of difference (Braidotti, 2022). This offers a compelling alternative to the negative imperative and cynicism of post-modernism and advanced capitalism, which seems more necessary than ever.

4 Affecting Femininities: The Principle of Not One

I'm a detective investigating myself. I try to be rigorous in my understanding of what happens to me and try to understand how to harness and change my unique story through theatre. In terms of staging femininity, you have to remember that I didn't start directing until my 30s. I'd been a woman for some time, knew and loved many women – and I had many frustrations about my female experience! When I finally felt the power in my hands and in my heart it was a joy to reveal that beauty is nothing to do with the face or the body.

(Rice, 2022a)

Emma has been forthright about how her body of work reflects her experience as a woman – her emotional life, frustrations and desires. Categories of woman, femaleness and femininities unfurl and change shape throughout her productions, reflecting the mobility of these terms – expressing the multiple parts of her self. The sex/gender distinction, which dominated second-wave feminisms, is increasingly being challenged by critique that argues for its mutuality. Like Braidotti, I am keen to recognise the positivity of difference in sexuate states operating *beside* and through social/cultural representations (Braidotti, 2022).

As such, I view the gendered term 'woman' as an expansive category, socially constructed, where gender fluidity and gender-realignment shift assumptions about gender/sex normativity. Femininity describes behaviours that construct a gendered representation, performed by any human (cis-male, cis-female, trans male, trans female, gender neutral, gender fluid) or, indeed, non-human. I'm interested in the ways that Emma's staging of femininities continues to evolve – how her body of work affects and is affected by her biography, her own changing body and the bodies of her female performers.

In this section, I consider groups of stories as feminist constellations, staging femininities and affecting feelings of pleasure and pain, often, but not always, in relation to love. Feminist constructs such as Luce Irigaray's feminist masquerade (Irigaray, 1985 p. 77), Rosi Braidotti's 'vital materialism' (Braidotti, 2011) and feminist readings of desire (Lorde,1984) offer ways to view this work. In thinking through Emma's shifting femininities it seems necessary to foreground the female performer's experience, to question how embodied action affects and the extent to which it is potentially transformative. This rarely shared perspective is vital if we are to recognise representation as a collaboration *between* director and performer. Patrycja Kujawska, Emma's collaborator for over two decades, has performed in nine productions. In Section 4.3, she reflects on the embedded and embodied affect of two moments of performed femininities from seminal feminist works: *Don John* (2009) and *Wild Bride* (2011).

4.1 Selkies and Sirens, Big Pants and Top Birds

Emma's feminist influences include Tracey Emin, Pina Bausch, Louise Bourgeois, Joan Littlewood and Angela Carter, all artists who, like Emma, 'dance their own dance'.[20] Thinking about their commonalities with broad brushstrokes is interesting: they are all experimental, anti-establishment, irreverent, fervent feminists – either radical, socialist or both – they work with heightened theatricality and magical realism. Their work stops you in your tracks. It changes the way you breathe, makes you feel awkward, embarrassed, scared, lost, angry, makes you laugh; they question constructs of power and mechanisms of control; their work makes us feel smaller or larger than we are; it disorientates. Most importantly, these artists tell stories which make us think about where we have been and where we are going, our place *in relation with* the constellations of life.

As a feminist constellation, Emma's stories can be grouped in particular firmaments, recognising that some appear in more than one. When we think

---

[20] In *Red Shoes* Lady Lydia ends the play with the line, 'And my secret's reserved for those/ Who dare to dance a different dance/With me'. *The Kneehigh Anthology: Volume 1* (Oberon Books, London, 2005).

about her body of work as an extension of her own body, each grouping reflects periods of her life, emotional memories creating a patchwork of experiences. There is her work for younger audiences, which questions how to be a girl, drawing on fairy tales, from authors such as Hans Christian Anderson, Michael Morpurgo and Enid Blyton. These include *Rapunzel* (2007), *Midnight's Pumpkin* (2012), *946: The Amazing Story of Adolphus Tips* (2016), *The Little Matchgirl* (2016) and *Mallory Towers* (2019). Emma's sense of *being* a girl – the longing, the dreaming, the transgressions, the anxiety, the secrets – pervades her work. She has said that the loss of her best friend at eleven left an indelible mark on her life when grief descended on her childhood: 'I was looking for somewhere to express grief and joy. This is what theatre gives me to this day' (Rice qtd in Kellaway, 2018). Then there are romantic love stories, the couple as protagonist, with the classic structure where they fight to be together against the odds or accept the tragedy of their enforced separation: *Tristan and Yseult* (2006), *A Matter of Life and Death* (2007), *Brief Encounter* (2009), *The Umbrellas of Cherbourg* (2011), *The Flying Lovers* (2016), *Romantics Anonymous* (2017) and *Wuthering Heights* (2022). Emma has described herself as 'very good at falling in love ... truly, madly, deeply' and these intoxicating stories reflect her as an incurable romantic (Kellaway, 2018). As a trained actor she has experienced the exhilaration and rejection of the profession. There are stories that explicitly place the female performer centre stage: *Pandora's Box* (2002), *Wah Wah Girls,* (2012), *Nights at the Circus* (2005) and *Wise Children* (2018). And revelation tales, where the protagonist comes to a point of new understanding, learn to be in her own skin: *Rebecca* (2015), *Bagdad Café* (2021) and *Wise Children* (2018). Whilst any one of these groupings offer rich pickings, here I focus on stories about female endurance and about being 'bad' (Rice, 2015a). Both strands explore psychophysical transformation through affecting pleasure and pain, bodily knowledge that Braidotti describes as carnal empiricism (2015a, p. 108).

Emma is drawn to folk stories of selkies, seal women who shed their seal skins to marry a human and then end up returning to their instinctive self and the ocean, reclaiming their rightful skin and leaving human duty behind. The image of a woman filmed swimming underwater is repeated in *Pandora's Box* (2002) and *Brief Encounter* (2009), but it is in her trilogy of fairy tale/folk tales – *The Red Shoes* (2001/2), *The Wooden Frock* (2003/4) and *Wild Bride* (2011/13) – that transformation is actualised. These stories reflect her own life-changing periods of emotional change: her divorce, new relationship and career as a director. They lead us through adaptation, striving to follow your heart and be true to yourself. In Brechtian fashion they all tell 'The Girl's' story, with innocence and joy consumed by male desire and violence. The female body is destined to endure – abused and battered, forced into servitude, forced into hiding. From physical mutilation and entrapment comes the body's ability to transform: in *The Red Shoes* her feet are cut off, in *The Wild Bride* her hands and in *The Wooden Frock* she is locked in the equivalent of chastity armour to prevent her bereaved father from taking advantage of her. Emma doesn't shy away from the affect of staging physical violence. Kneehigh's productions would often contain fight sequences but, in her staging of gendered violence, she confronts the shattering of female bodies and psyches. At times the grotesque undercuts these moments: mutilations are staged with an explosion of red ribbons to represent the spurting blood; in *The Wild Bride,* the child abuse of The Girl, by The Devil, is represented through a movement composition where he plays her like a musical instrument, to a twanging refrain. These stagings, like the tone of the original stories, simultaneously draw us in and alienate. The struggle and endurance of the performers' bodies is another factor that affects our sensitivity to pain. We feel the human stakes *through* their bodies – the exhaustion, the sweat, the desperation. There is the resonance of Polish sacrifice here, an echo of Grotowski, where the performers push their bodies through exhausting movement sequences, singing with an abandon and desperation, playing instruments with urgency and compunction. The physical expression of female endurance – the need to survive – pervades Emma's work and, as we shall see, is symptomatic of a process where, paradoxically, the performer's sacrifice can be liberating.

Whilst many stories pursue love as salvation, they are imbricated in the dialectic between social convention and free will, with bodies inscribed and inscribing. Emma has commented on how, whilst she has been brought up to be good, kind and moral, she is inextricably drawn to the opposite. She describes this strand of her work as 'the bad girl' stories that include myths: *The Bacchae* (2004), *Pandora's Box* (2002), legends, *Tristan and Yseult* (2006), *Don John* (2008) and feminist novels *Nights at the Circus* (2005) and *Wuthering Heights* (2022). These are stories of 'unruly women', choosing to follow their desires and be wild sirens, performing femininities to get what they want. Emma reflects on how telling stories about transgressions connects to her own love stories, 'I'm haunted by some of the choices that I've made. Unable to change history I try to manage the fallout of these choices with loyalty and kindness and love. But some carry a weight of responsibility that can feel hard to bear. How do you balance your moral compass with the wild woman inside you?' (Rice, 2022).

Wild women, intoxicated by desire, is another affecting trope. In *Tristan and Yseult* (2006, 2013, 2015), *Brief Encounter* (2009) and *Romantics Anonymous* (2017), the lovers, in sexual ecstasy, swing from chandeliers, defying gravity through the sheer exhilaration and force of joyful desire. Seeing this affects your body. You feel a childish glee, a whooping exuberance, your heartbeat increases, your body softens and you smile. In *Wise Children* there were nine sexual encounters. Emma enjoyed trying to pinpoint the kind of sex – the potential comedy of 'the quick shag' compared to the tenderness of desire (Rice, 2022). Across her oeuvre she 'works a lot with knickers' (Rice, 2022). Actors wear gym-type 'big pants', functional as opposed to sexy, drawing attention to the mechanics of the body. Taking off knickers is a repeated gesture – *Don John* (2008), *Tristan and Yseult* (2006), *Wise Children* (2022), *A Midsummer Night's Dream* (2016) highlighting the physical, everyday, comic/tragic reality of sex. She doesn't shy away from staging the messy, uncomfortable reality of the female body. In *Wise Children*, the twins get red knickers when they start their periods and we witness the pain of miscarriage; in *Tristan and Yseult*, after she has had sex with King Mark, Brangian, played by Craig Johnson, wipes herself between the legs to remove the sperm.

Emma likes to show skin on stage, its textures and imperfections, commenting, 'I like women to be beautiful for who they are, so I try very hard to portray women truthfully, not turned out, not fully toned, all shapes and sizes, natural' (Rice, 2015). The leading ladies or 'top birds' that she works with repeatedly – Annette McLoughlin, Dot Attkinson, Lizzie Winkler, Katy Owen, Tamzin Griffin, Mandy Lawrence, Beck Appleby, Éva Magyar, Nandi Bhebhe and Patrycja Kujawska – challenge normative representations through their body shapes, their height, strength, gangling clumsiness or unabashed enthusiasm. These are women 'voraciously in their own skins. They devour the world around them and there's a greed for experience, which is so outward looking that they'll do anything. . . . Their bellies are out!' (Rice, 2022a).

These performers are multi-disciplined actor/musicians, dancers or circus performers. 'Doing anything' requires a playfulness, an ability to be spontaneous and, particularly in the case of Katy Owen, to clown. Indeed, as important as exploring women's wildness is showing their ability to be funny, something Emma exploits and which, in Owen, she has found a muse. The bodily felt pleasure of performance is another affecting trope. In her staging we never remain in one emotional state for long. Sadness, loss or the shock of violence are interrupted with songs, musical numbers, comedy and dance. The audience experiences a patchwork of affects, a changeability, which puts the body in a state of readiness – readiness to succumb to the story and to be open to its humanity. Music, of course, is an important material in relation to the body and affect. The female body, singing and dancing, swinging from a trapeze, performing cartwheels or doing magic tricks is working *in relation with* the music as a powerful affecter of mood.

4.2 Shifting Femininities

Femaleness has long been associated with multiplicity, a destabilising force (Freud, 2018; Lacan, 1949 or doubled through constant self-surveillance (De Beauvoir, 1997; Diamond, 1997). New materialist feminisms explore the 'principle of not one', how the body is never only one thing: culture affects *beside* nature, bodies are inscribed *and* inscribing, embodied *and* embedded, in states of becoming – producing 'a vital materialism' (Braidotti, 2011). At this time of posthuman acceleration, feminisms look beyond social constructivist and linguistic turns that have stymied change, to recognise how 're-naturalisation and de-naturalization are intermeshed' as 'an active reconstruction of trans species, trans corporeal and transversal heterogeneous assemblages' (Braidotti, 2022, p. 136). This expands materialism as we think about bodies, femaleness and femininity, in new ways.

During her career, Emma has enlisted bodies in particular ways to tell stories that ask us to think about subject and community formations – drawing attention to gender as a biopolitical mechanism of control, where bodies have power imposed on them but also wield their own power. Carnal empiricism is a way of coming to understand these mechanisms. The critical feminist constructs of 'feminine mimicry', 'jouissance' and 'vital materialism' help to illuminate the impact of affecting femininities in performance.

Emma's stories show women performing their womanliness. In 1929, Joan Riviere's 'female masquerade' considered 'womanliness' as a mask, performed in defence to male power (Heath, 1985, pp.45–61). Luce Irigaray, seeking the agency in this, developed the idea of 'feminine mimicry' as an act of resistance. She suggests that women should 'play with mimesis ... assume the feminine role deliberately. Which means already to convert a form of subordination into an affirmation, and thus, begin to thwart it' (Irigaray, 1985 p. 77). The excess of performed femininity turns masquerade into mimicry and so ironises the constructed feminine ideal. The deliberate acting out of prescribed femininity reveals its hidden mechanisms. Elin Diamond explains this as a form of feminist gestic criticism (Diamond, 1997, p. xiv). Across the constellations of Emma's work, I see feminine mimicry used as a strategy to perform female power.

The feminine gest can be particularly powerful when performed by a different sex. Ben Spatz, in his consideration of gender as technique, suggests that this makes it more visible (Spatz, 2015, p. 171). An example of this can be seen in *Tristan and Yseult* (2006). Brangian, Yseult's maid, played by Craig Johnson, takes Yseult's place on her wedding night, losing her virginity to King Mark, in order to maintain the secret of her infidelity with Tristan. At this point there is a split stage with both couples having sex, downstage and upstage of each other. After the act, and before a heartfelt monologue, Brangian turns upstage, takes a washcloth and wipes between her legs to remove the sperm. Such a feminine gest at this moment, when played by a man, both draws you into the tragedy – the female body, in all its material reality, used as transaction, and the emotional impact of that – and alienates you. Emma's sensitive direction, telling Johnson, 'If anyone in the audience laughs or titters just catch their eye and make it as honest as possible', produced a heartbreaking moment of affecting vulnerability whilst simultaneously asserting the inscribing mechanisms of control on female bodies (Johnson, 2022).

Female power is connected to the erotic and to sexual pleasure. Black feminist love politics harnesses the erotic as a necessary feminist source of power. Audre Lorde, in her 1984 essay, 'Uses of the Erotic. The Erotic as Power' states

> For the erotic is not a question only of what we do; It is a question of how acutely and fully we *feel* [my italics] in the doing. Once we know the extent to which we are capable of feeling that sense of satisfaction and completion, we can then observe which of our various life endeavours brings us closest to that fullness (Lorde, 2017, p. 24).

In this way, the erotic becomes a feminist strategy for change through affirmative politics. As I noted, the pleasure and pain of sex is a feature of Emma's stories but beyond the representation of female desire is the *how* of the playing. As an audience we feel the erotic as a quality when we see a performer play with abandon, dance and sing with elation, or feel the shared rhythm and resonance of the ensemble. Jouissance is a slippery term associated with an excess of pleasure, which, like Kirstu Lempiäinen, I see as a quality of feminist materialism through relational becoming. I become an 'I' *because of* the presence of others that share the same pleasurous space (Lempiäinen, 2010, p. 112). This felt sense of jouissance is transmitted through the energies of Emma's performers.

Her stories of transformation – of bodies and psyches – go to the heart of Braidotti's posthuman feminist project that refigures humanism to recognise that we are in a constant state of becoming – in relation *with* space, people, technology, animals, objects. This builds on feminist technoscience, LGTBQ+ theories, Black, colonial and indigenous feminisms to configure a different sense of subjectivity and a vital materialism (Braidotti, 2022). Emma's performers work with the non-human (instruments, puppets, costumes, objects; see Section 3.2 on 'thing-ness') to affect transformation through co-constitutive intra-activity between human and non-human agents. Simultaneously, transversal affect happens *within* the body. When we think beyond external representation to the atoms and cells in constant diffractive interactions, internal affect comes into play, expanding its reach.

In pursuing my imperative to widen the scope of affect beyond the experience of the audience, it seems vital to include the performer's point of view. How does the performer herself experience the potential of transversal affect in staging femininities? Using these feminisms as a lens I focus on the work of performer Patrycja Kujawska, considering the affects of performance moments from two productions, *Don John* (2009) and *The Wild Bride* (2011), that highlight shifting femininities – female endurance and being 'bad'. Kujawska, re-watching these moments on video, recalls her own bodily felt sense.

4.3 An Actress Affects

In 2007, Emma saw Patrycja Kujawska performing in Sheffield with the feminist Charlotte Vincent Theatre Dance Company and was, perhaps, returned to the unbound emotion of Polish company Gardzienice. Kujawska is a multi-disciplined artist, captivating in her movement and virtuosic in her musicianship. She has played the violin since she was seven, with classical training at the Academy of Music in Poland. To my mind, alongside Katy Owen's playful and peerless comic sensibility, Kujawska encapsulates the quality of Emma's 'top birds' – individual, fearless, passionate and generous – able to switch from affecting pain to joyful pleasure in a heartbeat.

Kujawska has worked with Emma on eight productions, first with Kneehigh and subsequently Wise Children (*Don John*, 2008; *The Wild Bride*, 2011; *The Red Shoes*, 2010; *Tristan and Yseult*, 2013; *Midnights Pumpkin* 2012; *946: The Amazing Story of Adolphus Tips*, 2016; *Wise Children*, 2018; and *Bagdad Café*, 2021) and with Mike Shepherd in *Dead Dog in a Suitcase (and other love songs)* (2019). She is committed to feminist work, maintaining her fourteen years collaboration because the stories speak to her politics and she gets to flex new muscles as a performer. At the risk of stating the obvious, each role presents different types of transformation, affecting her body-matter. In *946*, she had to disguise her pregnant state. In *Bagdad Café*, she worked with an accent coach, speaking in English and shifting her Polish accent to German. She now reflects that, in the 180 ferocious performances of The Girl in *The Red Shoes* (2010/11), she was exorcising her own personal pain. The fact that the role required her to have a shaved head became a psychological challenge. Unlike a costume she could remove, she was stuck with the bodily transformation throughout the run – carrying the angst of the character into her every day. Over fourteen years her own cis-female body, in its constant states of becoming, continues to reveal new possibilities. The following two moments of performance, selected from 'bad girl' and endurance stories, illustrate and illuminate affecting femininities.

Don John (2009), a collaboration between Kneehigh and the RSC, was, in many ways, speaking to a feminism before its time. Adapted by Emma, with text by Anna Marie Murphy, music by Stu Barker, designed by Vicki Mortimer and inspired by the Mozart/Da Ponte Don Giovanni, the story was re-imagined in a small country town in 1979, during the Winter of Discontent in Thatcherite Britain, to a background of strikes and power cuts. This retelling, reclaimed for the female characters, follows the stories of three women (an elegant business-women, an alcoholic vicar's wife and a bookish Polish cleaner) who fall victim to the sexual predator.

The adaptation, which critic Michael Billington derided as 'shadowed by a masterpiece', bemoaning its comparative 'loss of terror' (2008), speaks loudly to the political mood in 2022, and feminist uprisings against sexual violence. Billington's gendered response perhaps reveals how, for him, the effect of the story is diminished when the gaze shifts from male to female. Indeed, Emma recalls how, in rehearsal, when Icelandic actor, Gísil Örn Garðarsson, playing 'protagonist' Don John, was necessarily absent for a week, the process seam-lessly moved forward without him, as he was an adjunct to the main storylines. In a chilling sequence, John's sidekick, Nobby, played by Mike Shepherd, who keeps an audit of John's sexual conquests, plays a slide show of their photo-graphs to a song titled *Wantonness*. We are reminded of the ongoing lists of sexual victims, added to every day, in perpetuum, and the framings of sexual violence. Utilising the industrial set, made up of shipping containers festooned with fairy lights, the chorus, the all-female dance group Seascape, graffitied their own lists, the names of women they loved, to the sound of the 1962 Crystals track *He hit me (and it felt like a kiss)*.

Kujawska, playing Zerlina, the Polish cleaner, wearing impractical red plat-forms, succumbs to her desire and is seduced by John the night before her wedding to the affable Alan, played by Craig Johnson. The performance of female desire and transgression in this moment, through its sexual gymnastics, encapsulates the pleasure and pain of 'the bad girl' stories. In trying to commu-nicate its affect I write in the present tense:

The lower section of the stage is lit with festoons. The onstage band plays a seductive number *Sweet Lies* throughout the sequence, overlayed with dra-matic action. A wedding cake is centre stage on a table. The dancers move to the side of the stage and continue moving as the scene is set for a seventies disco. The seduction is simultaneously exciting, and disturbingly familiar. I recognise the 'feminine masquerade': the lovers stand on opposite sides of the room, Zerlina smoking seductively, taking off her high heels to stand, off balance, hip out, nonchalant. Physical contact starts with the ingenious removal and swap-ping of coats, teasing weapons which flick, stroke, tickle; then moves to lifts and holds, lips tantalisingly close. In a performance of power, which I cringe to recall in my own behaviour, Don John recoils from her, making her pursue him. She stops him leaving with her foot on his back, pulls him to the floor, pinning him beneath her. The slow-motion simulation of foreplay in half-light is intercut with flashes of comic dialogue from the vicar 'Today's sermon is about love'. The pleasure and pain of the transgression is layered with dark humour.

There is powerful chemistry between the performers, the handsome Garðarsson, now in his white vest and black leather trousers, oozes sexiness. As Don John lifts Zerlina towards the table, pushes the wedding cake to the floor and takes her from standing position, her legs are comically, tragically, spread-eagled. After John has left, during the next scene, Zerlina remains on her back on the table in spotlight, red knickers showing and long legs dangling. This paralysis of post coital pleasure turns on an edge the longer she remains motionless. Confronted with the image, I shift from the exhilaration of the transgressive to disquiet, then to disgust. I think of the women who never regain consciousness.

Kujawska reflects:

> Stu Barker's track 'Desire', underscoring this scene, does something to your body to immediately make you feel sexy. I (Zerlina) never felt like a victim. I (Zerlina) never felt ashamed. She was not a silly girl. She consciously allowed herself to be seduced. Zerlina is in the moment, living her life to the full. She takes ownership of her mistakes. How rarely do we see on the stage women who are unapologetic in betraying and making mistakes?
>
> Emma gave us a task: 'You have to have sex during the length of the song. Think about it as a dance' and that's all she said. And because Garðarsson is an ex gymnast we knew that we could use his strength and my flexibility, and have fun with it, not make it too obvious and too explicit, but more ambiva-lent. Except the last image, [on the table] which is when the music stops, lights are changing, it's unpleasant and ugly. Lying there I remember enjoying that moment, enjoying the shift and the repulsive shock I sensed in the audience. (2022)

My second example, *The Wild Bride*, was at The Lyric Hammersmith in 2011–12, then toured the United Kingdom, the United States and Australia in 2013. Emma revisited an earlier production, *The Handless Maiden*, based on the German folktale by The Brothers Grimm, that she had made in Budapest, Hungary, with Éva Magyar. In this iteration she collaborated with three extraordinary physical storytellers: Magyar, Kujawska and Audrey Brisson, all playing The Girl. Carl Grose wrote the text and Stu Barker the music. Emma reflects that, 'It was so close to my heart. So rooted in the earth, rooted in pain, rooted in truth, and yet in that magical language that I love, the folktale' (Rice, 2020). The Girl's hapless alcoholic father, played by Stuart Goodwin, unwittingly sells her to The Devil, played by Stuart McLoughlin, who insists that he cuts off her hands as he can't be touched by her purity. The story follows The Girl at three stages of her life: she escapes the Devil, lives in the wild, finds love, learns to use 'Edward Scissor Hands' prosthetics, has a child and, due to the Devil's trickery, is forced to return to the wilds where, eventually, her hands regrow and she is reunited with her love. It was set in depression-era America with a rough aesthetic, reminiscent of Kneehigh's earlier works, a gnarly tree upstage, from which the Devil narrates, singing to a blues score. In this story, which speaks to female endurance and transformation, I am drawn to the vital materialism of the female body, it's inherent 'principle of not one', 'naturalising queerness, queering nature' (Braidotti, 2020, p. 176). Critic Lyn Gardner suggested, 'this is a show not just to be seen but also to be felt' (2011). I feel my way through Kujawska's performance of transformation into 'the wild' (see Figure 4).

The transition between the first and second stage of The Girl's story is marked by Brisson, the youngest iteration, who sings a moody blues number, *Down at the Crossroads*, with gravely vocals, accompanied by Kujawska, playing violin in half darkness. At the song's finale, stepping into the light, she plays the most extraordinary virtuosic solo, working the instrument with such ferocity that I get goosebumps – the violin screeching and crying like a dying animal. Kujawska's body resonates through the instrument, inextricably joined. Magyar and Brisson take it from her, change her clothes and bind her hands to demonstrate the passing between selves. The removal of her violin feels like another mutilation.

The forest floor is covered in leaves, the Devil watching from above, Brisson on mic, accompanied by live strings and recorded noises, creating a wailing siren-like underscore. Kujawska, in a three-minute movement sequence working with Magyar, transforms into 'the wild'. As Magyar operates a deer puppet, Kujawska mirrors the animal's movement and rhythms, twitching her neck to the side, raising her shoulders, finding a lightness in her spine and in her feet, jerking, jumping, scratching twisting, leaping, aided by Magyar as an invisible force, shaping her body into the four-legged-hoof-ness and lightness of the deer. Kujawska canters around the space in circles, her fists making tight circles, dropping to the floor, twisting, writhing and, at intervals, Magyar covers her with dirt, until she shifts into something non-human, finally placing a crown of twigs on her head. Her shape is other-worldly. Kujawska's movement, working with fluid spine, impulse and energy, captures Polish movement practice, its connection to the earth and the life force. It makes me feel breathless, angry, desperate for her survival, captivated by the power of her body, its extraordinary ability to transform.

Figure 4 Patrycja Kujawska in *The Wild Bride* (2012)
Photo courtesy of Steve Tanner

Kujawska reflects:

> It starts with a song, which is absolutely brilliant, and you don't know what's going to happen. You don't know how you can be transported from the bluesy, raunchy, painfully beautiful singing of Audrey, and me cracking a violin solo, to such brutality. And it's such condensed brutality, so simple, so big and intense at times, like thick brush strokes.
>
> I remember the task – for the duration of the song you have to go from being a brutalized girl without hands, to become wild and free – that's the journey over three minutes. So I was improvising forever, and I was sore and

bruised. We choreographed it as a circular shape of movement. We had a soft floor with a carpet underlay so I could throw myself on my knees and do this kind of funny thing of standing on my toes curled up because it was all protected. That required a particular kind of physical strength, to act that as well as move. Somehow the transformation, what I was feeling – what my muscles were doing, in my bones, things were growing on and in me to become stronger. It was quite visceral and that was an exhausting element of the transformation.

When I look at the video now the stage seems so much smaller. It really felt so big for me and (as the character) I'm on such a journey. I could really recall that journey despite it being ten years ago. I'm surprised that I look strangely like a mixture of everything, vulnerable and girl-like and athletic, strong and women-like. It's so moving. What I'm seeing are all the girls, all the women. It's a such a symbolic archetypal journey; the transformation and the story of survival. (2022)

Emma's feminist body of work stages the principle of not one through the multiplicity of femininities and femaleness: the force of fragility, endurance, transformation, the power of the erotic and the tragi-comedy of the everyday. The female body misbehaves, falls apart and holds together in messy, vulnerable, heart-warming magnificence. The stories respond to her own biography, her bodily felt sense as wild woman, lover, bad girl, siren, selkie and clown. We can see these archetypes as projections of her own multiple femininities, her 'top birds' collaborating as alter-egos.[21] Importantly, Kujawska's reflections remind us that, for the performer, the self is always doubled, both 'authentic' and performed, enacted and embodied, affected and affecting.

5 Affecting Queer Worldmaking: Casting

Casting is something that's developed and evolved over my career. Sometimes I cast by mistake, sometimes because of tight budgets but more and more my choices are made because of the political power that these vital decisions have. My casting has become an illustration of my belief that we are all capable of anything. We are all capable of being amazing and of being dreadful. I love to stir the archetypal pot and surprise myself with cliché busting leaps of radical faith. As artists and human beings, let's see if we can all be the best version of ourselves as much as possible.

(Rice, 2022b)

At the time of writing, recent events have called to account wide-scale systemic institutional prejudice. We are experiencing an explosion of identity politics – pushing against racism, sexism, classism, ableism, ageism. In theatre, casting

---

[21] Thanks to Duška Radosavljević for this suggestion. In conversation with the author 30 November 2022.

functions as a tool of discursive power that can expose, resist and reform representations of identity, reaching towards Jill Dolan's 'new humanism' – a re-invigorated democracy (2005, p. 21). When we think about Emma's evolving approach to casting through the lens of posthuman feminisms, loosening unitary identities and binaries, it becomes a radical strategy, aligned with Rosi Braidotti's assertion, '"We"-who-are-not-one-and-the-same-but-are-in-*this*-together' (2022, p. 8).

The Equality Act in the United Kingdom, protecting workers on nine counts of identity discrimination, came into play in 2010. However, as Aston notes, there remains a stubbornly slow movement towards changing the status quo in the theatre industry. Despite media coverage, which suggests the gap is narrowing, data sets, compiled by the industry, show that the percentage gains for women in all areas have been achingly slow, remaining in single figures over the past ten years. Aston, highlighting how the 2014 Arts Council of England's funding model for NPO's (National Portfolio Organisations) favoured almost twice as many male CEOS – 63 per cent (119) male directors compared to 37 per cent (69 female directors) – states that without gender change at the top there will be little movement (Aston, 2020, p. 4). On the plus side, there is ongoing affirmative action from activist groups in the call to bring in quota systems, for example: ERA fifty–fifty (Equal Representation for Actresses) founded in 2015; Act for Change in 2014; and Tonic Theatre in 2011.[22] The Arts Council insisted that in the 2018–20 funding round NPO bids included an equality and diversity action plan (Aston, 2020). Such moves promise change; however, Aston's scepticism sounds loudly when comparing Emma's impact during her tenure as artistic director at The Globe, with that of Rufus Norris, artistic director of The National Theatre. In 2016, Norris committed to a fifty–fifty gender split for women directors and playwrights by 2021, a deadline which he has now extended (Dale, 2022). However, in 2019, before the Covid-19 pandemic hit, Norris was publicly lambasted for a male-dominated season. He admitted he had 'dropped the ball' (Hemming, 2019). Emma, on the other hand, who pledged fifty–fifty gender parity and 40 per cent Black and global majority casting, achieved this in her first year (2017). And did so from the eye of the storm, with Shakespeare's male-dominated canon.

Words like 'inclusivity' and 'diversity' can easily morph into performatives in institutional parlance. Whilst quota systems are one way of marking change, an over reliance on quantitative data can bely systemic prejudices, leaving marginalised people underrepresented in casting (Thompson, 2006; Rogers, 2019; Stamatiou, 2020). Stamatiou calls to attention the qualitative detail,

---

[22] ERA www.era5050.co.uk/; Act for Change https://en-gb.facebook.com/ActForChangeProject/; Tonic Theatre www.tonictheatre.co.uk/

such as whether the representation is positive or negative, that can insidiously perpetuate historical stereotypes. Citing Thompson, she explains how, in the sixties, the term 'integrated casting' gave way to 'inclusive casting', 'colour-blind' or 'colour-conscious' casting – terms that can be extended to gender (Thompson, 2006, pp. 6–7). There are four different types of inclusive casting practice: casting 'blind', regardless of race/gender/ability; societal casting, where actors with marginalised identities are cast in a variety of roles; conceptual casting, using a marginalised identity to make a point; and cross-casting culturally, which is setting the story in another culture (Stamatiou, 2020, pp. 3–4). Each approach is contextual and contingent, and, when we look at the detail, riddled with complications where inclusive casting can reaffirm the very systems it attempts to dismantle. Emma is aware of her responsibility in recognising the politics of casting: 'I hate the word colour blind casting. My eyes are wide open when I cast. What does this do? How does this challenge the audience?' (2022b). Roles need to move beyond stereotypical representations and certain tests have been devised to monitor this. For example, following the Bechdel test, the Sphinx test demands that a woman is 'centre stage driving the action in a culturally impactful drama'; the Fries test demands that a disabled character has their own narrative purpose (Aston, 2020, p. 18). Of course, we should be mindful that, for some, the promise that inclusive casting might help an audience confront their unconscious biases could be seen as peddling a naive utopia that sidesteps the reality of systemic and institutional discrimination.

In reality, there is a tension in casting for diversity when trying to maintain a long-standing company. When Kneehigh, a majority white male Cornish company, tried to diversify, they struggled to attract the much smaller pool of actors of colour to the 'pretty low grade' touring set-up (an ongoing issue for women with families) (Rice, 2022a). In 2011, the open call for *The Wild Bride* attracted no performers of colour. Emma reflects, 'It was hard to understand this new world. We really wanted to change and evolve but couldn't seem to make it happen. The challenge shone a light on who we were, where we made work, how we made work and how we toured' (Rice, 2022b). In 2012, *The Wah! Wah! Girls*, a Theatre Royal Stratford East production, in association with Kneehigh and Sadler's Wells, gave her the chance to expand her collaborators, working with Tanika Gupta, Niraj Chang, Tony Jayawardena and Natasha Jayetileke. Her move to The Globe in 2016, felt like 'an explosion', opening up 'a diverse global family' (Rice, 2022b). As stated, she achieved her pledge for gender equality and diversity within the first season. Emma wryly comments, 'The choices about equality and diversity happened easily and joyfully. As a woman, I thought 'Bloody hell! This is easy!' Once you've got power you can change the world really quickly. What I didn't expect was that I would get sacked within six months' (Rice, 2022b). Whilst, ostensibly, it was her insistence on using technology that caused the split, one could surmise that the pace of change, not least her approach to casting, may have contributed to the disquiet.

In her new company, the *Wise Children Mission Statement* foregrounds a commitment to diversity: through the casting, material, work with Wise Council (a group focussed specifically on broadening the diversity of audiences) and in the School for Wise Children, offering 'accessible and affordable training for a new and more diverse generation of practitioners'.[23] In 2022, 35 per cent of the workforce is from the global majority with fifty–fifty gender in all areas, making them a forerunner in the industry. Her casting continues to challenge representations. Enid Blyton's *Malory Towers* (2019) turned the expectation of white, middle-class, able-bodied girls on its head. Critic Afifa Akbar notes:

> In casting terms, Blyton's Malory girls now encompass difference and diversity, with two actors of colour (the excellent Izuka Hoyle as Darrell Rivers and Renée Lamb as Alicia), another who is non-binary (Vinnie Heaven as tomboy Bill Robinson) and one who has dwarfism (Francesca Mills, who plays Sally Hope with bossy brilliance). The cast are all equally magnificent, energetic performers with forceful, flawless voices (Akbar, 2010).

Emma's work, with its non-naturalistic style, requiring the audience to suspend their disbelief, opens up the possibilities of and potential for queering casting.

5.1 Queering Drag

Throughout her career Emma has bended gender. Her use of drag, from Lady Lydia in *The Red Shoes* (2001) to Dora Chance in *Wise Children* (2018), reflects the ways that theories and attitudes around gender and queer identities have shifted. Our cultural identity is produced through the performance of particular behaviours, where what we do becomes who we are. In the hands of a director, the specific body cast to perform a particular role, and how visible their performance of gender or ethnicity is either resists or reaffirms representations. In *Gender Trouble*, Judith Butler used drag as a way to question assumptions about a 'true gender' through parodying a primary gender identity (2006, p. 223). Whilst acknowledging that some feminist theorists, including bell hooks, saw drag as ridiculing, and thus degrading to women, Butler acknowledged that 'the relation between the "imitation" and the "original" was 'more complicated than that critique generally allows' (Butler, 2006, p. 224). In Butler's *Bodies that Matter*,

---

[23] Shared in correspondence.

'Ambivalent Drag' returned to this, drawing attention to the problematic reaffirm-ation of a heterosexual matrix, with its assumed binary of male/female, which reifies the inherently inscribed body. Butler asserts that every drag performance is unique; whilst for one, the transferability of a gender norm might call 'into question the abject in power that it sustains' for another, it might 'augment its hegemony through its denaturalisation' as 'there is no guarantee that exposing the naturalised status of heterosexuality will lead to its subversion' (1993, p. 205). For Butler, sexual difference comes into being through discursive practices and so sex and gender are mutually dependent. Emma's early work with drag can be considered from this perspective.

More recently, gender and queer theory seeks to disentangle 'assumptions about male and female' to recognise the multiplicity of gender technique which uniquely draws on particular aspects of sexual difference. Ben Spatz sees gender as the foundation, with sex, sexuality and sexual difference as substrata, suggesting that we should 'fracture the very categories of male and female, masculine and feminine' in order to develop 'male femininities and female masculinities' (Spatz, 2015, p. 187). We now experience numerous divergent approaches to gender and so 'new gender technique and new gender communi-ties' need to be fostered (Spatz, 2015, p. 211). Similarly, for Rosi Braidotti's posthuman feminism, gender and sex are relational and co-implicated. She looks beyond these parameters to a 'process of differing' where 'sexuality comes *before* gender [my italics], because matter is sexuate'; it 'mutates and moves' and so 'being sexual means to be endowed with multiple sexual morphologies' (2022, p. 183). This principle of not one offers a strategic de-territorialisation for identity categories and I apply this thinking to Emma's later work on casting in *Wise Children*.

In *Queering Drag: Redefining the Discourse of Gender Bending*, Meredith Heller calls for a more nuanced, less essentialist discourse on drag to question why certain acts reaffirm the status quo and others, citing Berlant and Warner, enable 'queer worldmaking' to build new gender communities (2020, p. 5). Heller opens up the boundaries of what constitutes a 'bent' practice to include 'any act that is out 'of sync with the hegemonic framework', focussing on women's gender bending, which, she argues, is more 'effective at creating lasting macro-cultural gender shifts' and 'large scale gender dismantling' because the performances are 'less alienating' and 'more subtle' (2020, p. 29). In her overview of the canon of drag theory, Heller points to the conflict of feminist theorists who, like Diamond, either see drag as a type of Brechtian gestus critiquing feminine oppression or who, like Dolan, see it as an inevitable reification of the superior male gender position (2020, p. 25). Reiterating Spatz, Heller's problem with this is the reaffirmation of the sex–gender binary, and binary sex categories in Western culture. For Heller, 'Ideally, any discussion about the bending of gender would be foundationally built on how a body's bent expression calls specific gender meanings into question. In this ideological frame, 'bending gender actually bends the parameters of gender taxonomies rather than simply allowing a subject to rehearse them' (2020, p. 17). This, I go on to argue, is what Emma's approach to casting starts to enable.

In what ways does drag affect? How does it make us feel? Of course, this is subjective and uniquely experienced but there is, perhaps, some common ground. Alongside the most obvious affect of comedy – laughing at the alternative – is the intertwined affect of shame. Eve Sedgwick harnesses the affect of 'shame dynamics' as inherent in political correctness and a particular feature of queer identities, an alternative to 'the recalcitrant notes that tie themselves into the guts of identity politics' (2003, p. 40). For Sedgwick, queer performativity is the performance of shame which 'mantles the threshold between introversion and extroversion, between absorption and theatricality, between performance and performativity' (2003, p. 38). I'm alert to the shame dynamics of Emma's queer performativity, mixing together comedy and tragedy, pleasure and pain, to produce the vital affect of compassion.

5.2 Towards Queer Worldmaking

I took very easily to men portraying women. It is deep in our cultural DNA and I often find it tender and revealing. It took me longer to find the right women to portray men, but I did. And of course, they did it brilliantly, with equal surprise and understanding. (Rice, 2016)

How can we assess the subtle and particular ways that drag affects? Heller identifies three particular modes of analysis for identification to offer a more nuanced consideration of gender bending: *revisionary identification* (as in changing the expected sex of casting, for example the Bacchants in *The Bacchae*, 2004); counter-identification or *cross-casting* (changing the gender identity of a role, for example Helenus as opposed to Helena in *A Midsummer Night's Dream*, 2016); *disidentification* (re-imagining gender, for example the multiple casting of the twins in *Wise Children*, 2018) (2020, p. 25). These three productions best illustrate (and problematise) Heller's categories and, in two of them, gender bending is crucial to the plot. A consideration of casting, language use and gestural technique reveals the evolution of Emma's bending practice. Here I'm focussing on male drag whilst acknowledging that, as Emma notes, there are plenty of examples of female drag in her more recent work, such as Katy Owen as Malvolio in *Twelfth Night* (2017). As Heller indicates, female drag could offer rich, and perhaps more subtle, vectors of analysis, for future research (2020, p. 29).

Emma's early work with drag reveals some contradictions and, recalling Butler, can be slightly ambivalent. For Kneehigh, a predominantly male company, casting, often pragmatic and multi-rolling, lent itself to drag, where 'big guys in frocks was funny' (Rice, 2015). That said, in 2002, her landmark and award-winning production, *The Red Shoes*, by Anna Marie Murphy, was narrated by Lady Lydia, played by Giles King, as an ex-soldier in drag, with a chorus of three white-faced, shaved-headed men in dirty vests and y-fronts, representing the wartime cowards in the First World War. Lydia's final reveal was 'And my secret's reserved for those/ Who dare to dance a different dance:/ With me'.[24] Emma's first use of drag presents the complexity of the lived, alternative queer experience – parodic *and* alienating, transgressive *and* painfully risky.

The Bacchae (2005), written by Carl Grose and Anna Marie Murphy, winner of the TMA award for the best touring production, is an illustration of *revisionary identification* where drag can be ambivalent. The Bacchantes were men, bare-chested, in tutus (see Figure 5). An archived document, perhaps directed at funders, 'Kneehigh Theatre *The Bacchae* 2004' overviews the production concept. Here, Emma justifies her idea for casting:

Figure 5 Bacchantes in *The Bacchae* (2005)

Photo courtesy of Steve Tanner

---

[24] *The Red Shoes* written by Anna Maria Murphy, in *The Kneehigh Anthology: Volume 1* (Oberon Modern Play, London, 2005) p. 202.

My Bacchae will be all men. In fact the whole cast will be male. This choice is also at the heart of the production and the process. ... I want to look at femininity afresh and I want my audience to do the same. With a male cast they can look in at femininity and reinvent it for themselves. They will be more womanly than women.[25]

This position, recalling Brecht, works with gestic femininity, where gender as technique exposes its performativity and illuminates the mechanisms of control on bodies (Diamond, 1997). Alternatively, one could argue that the materiality of female bodies is required to explode those power structures. When you give the possibility of an act of female transgression to a chorus of male bodies, what is gained and what is lost? Perhaps an entirely male company might have communicated more clearly but, in casting Éva Magyar as Agave, whose toplessness in the Mountain orgy mirrored the bare-chested chorus, there was, to my mind, some slightly confused signalling in a story where queering is presented simultaneously as hedonistic activism and as terrorism.

The staging of scenes 13 and 14, where the stage directions call for '*wild abandon*', '*a Bacchic orgy*' leading to the killing of Pentheus, '*the Bacchae pour wine over Pentheus' face, beat him and tear his pants off*', with Agave '*topless, wearing a red tutu and covered in blood*' as '*The Bacchae become monsters*',[26] was powerfully affecting. Ian Watson noted the influence of Gardzienice in the physicality, ritual and music (Watson, 2004). The shift from parody to transgression and violent transformation was palpable but male bodies performing violence is received differently, and, ultimately, the threat of female power is clouded. Almost two decades later, both Emma and Craig Johnson, leader of the Bacchant chorus, acknowledge that this casting would be problematic now, particularly in terms of taking roles away from female performers (Rice, 2015; Johnson, 2022). At the time, queering roles didn't ignite the same ethical and political scrutiny and it served the needs of the company. One could argue that such circumstances were generative for Emma's subsequent evolvement in queering drag.

When Emma joined The Globe, the first production she directed in the 'Wonder Season' was *A Midsummer Night's Dream* (2016), with Tanika Gupta as dramaturg. This production offers an example of *cross-casting*. Her pledge for diversity and equality was made manifest in and through her casting. Parsee Indian British actor Zubin Varla played Oberon and Theseus to white Australian performer Meow Meow's Titania and Hippolyta. Anjana Vasan as Hermia and Ankur Bahl as Helenus both had Indian South Asian Heritage, alongside 'Hoxton hipsters', Black actor, Ncuti Gatwa as Demetrius and white

---

[25] Accessed at Falmouth Archive (8 September 2022).
[26] *The Bacchae* written by Carl Grose, in *The Kneehigh Anthology: Volume 1* (Oberon Modern Play, London, 2005) pp. 111–3.

actor and Edmund Derrington as Lysander. The counter-identification or cross-casting came with the all-female mechanicals (bar Nic Bottom, played by Ewan Wardrop), Katy Owen as Puck and Helena shifting to Helenus.

Changing the gender and sexuality of such a seminal female juvenile lead was a radical move. In doing so, Emma confronted Helena's problematic absolution of Demetrius at the end of the play, easily forgiving his previously violent treatment of her. By switching gender, Demetrius' aggressive behaviour can be seen to be caused by frustrated and repressed sexuality, remembering Sedgwick, his queer shame. In the programme note Emma comments, 'By making it a gay relationship I understand why he has been pushing Helenus away and why he feels the social pressure to make a good marriage. I also understand why, at the end, Demetrius says he has returned to his 'natural taste'' (2016). In the programme, Bruce Smith, in *Queer Goings On*, reminds us that sex/gender distinctions are contextual and explain how the play 'touches on territories we would call queer' (Smith, 2016). In the sixteenth century there were different understandings of sex and sexuality: sex might be with plants and animals; there were more convictions for bestiality than rape and no one 'located personal identity in sexual preference' (Smith, 2016). Of course, at this time, there would have been all male casts. Emma's casting, in its fluidity and polymorphous states, references the original whilst speaking to contemporary gender politics. Her use of songs, punctuating the action throughout, underlines this. Oberon and Titania's final song, playing on Puck's earlier line 'Jack shall have Jill/ Naught shall go ill',[27] was characteristically playful and provoking:

Oberon: Jack shall have Jill
             Jill shall have Jack
             Naught shall go ill
             There's no looking back …
Titania: Jill shall have Jill
             Jack shall have Jack
             No one will need
             An aphrodisiac[28]

Susanna Clapp described the production as a 'glittering, unnerving comic triumph' (2016). Whilst it was widely commended for its playful wildness, its reflection of multicultural contemporary London and its bold rethinking of gender and sexuality, there were dissenting voices. Some took umbrage with the 'school disco' effect of the lighting and sound as non-authentic for The

---

[27] Act 3, sc 2, lines 463-464.
[28] Zubin Varla (Oberon) and Meow Meow (Titania) *A Midsummer Night's Dream*, The Globe, 2016.

Globe (Morrison, 2016). Kate Maltby pointed to the lack of eroticism in the production and how, with a male Bottom, Emma's cross-gendered casting was 'behind the times' (Maltby, 2016). Hassana Moosa, whilst valuing the multi-cultural casting also perceived some 'appropriations that seemed to reproduce orientalist logics ... in order to evoke images of otherness' (Moosa, 2021). Ultimately, the reading of agency and power through the sex, gender, race, ability and age of bodies is subjective and relational. Crucially, I would argue that, in pushing against established representations, vital space is made for these questions.

The three male lovers – Lysander, Demetrius and Helenus – were presented as 'Hoxton Hipsters', referencing a trendy, young, demographic of East London. Helenus wore beige chinos, rolled up to above the ankles, with smart trainers, a white long-sleeved T-shirt and a grey blazer with rolled up sleeves. His unreciprocated love garnered compassion from the audience through his open and vulnerable characterisation, his camp and theatrical physicality, punctuated by exaggerated queening gestures, working with objects to perform queer as a gestic technique. In his first soliloquy, 'Love can transpose to form and dignity',[29] Helenus sat on the edge of the stage and held the hand of an audience member. When finding Lysander passed out in the forest, he took the first aid kit, worn as a bum bag, and proceeded to put on rubber gloves, which he later removed, and sanitised his hands.[30] In the heat of the argument with Hermia he applied lip balm to his lips, also offering it to Lysander and Demetrius, which Hermia then wiped onto his white shirt, much to his chagrin.[31] On the line 'She was a vixen when she went to school' Helenus sashayed to the front of the stage, with exaggerated swaying of his hips, a toss of his head and a click of his fingers, performing a queening gesture.[32] These actions were simultaneously funny and tragic as, returning to Sedgewick, Helenus was victim of Demetrius' shame in his denied sexuality. This elicited compassion, heard in the audible 'Awwws' from the audience, whenever Helenus was pained or humiliated.

How was Bahl, himself, affected by playing this role in these specific moments? He had previously worked with Emma on *The Empress* (2013) and, with her typically collaborative approach, they met to discuss the idea of cross-gendering Helena before she offered him the part. As a gay man, Emma wanted his take on the sensitivities of this radical casting decision with close attention to the text. After two hours of close scrutiny, they were united in their enthusiasm. In reflecting on the aforementioned moments, Bahl offers fascinating insight into the

---

[29] Act 1, sc1, lines 236–62.   [30] Act 2, sc2, line 760.   [31] Act 3, sc2.
[32] Act 3, sc2, line 1374.

decisions underpinning these gestures. The 'lip gloss' exchange was borne from the text itself and Hermia's 'painted maypole'[33] insult to Helenus; the sashaying 'vixen moment' was prompted by the rhythm and beat of the line. For Bahl, the role was empowering in a number of ways: he could build a contemporary interpretation which offered something new to the play, connecting with a predominantly young audience; and he was able to perform and celebrate aspects of his own identity, drawing on personal cultural references, to challenge heteronormativity. He commented:

> Some of the gestures I used in this production are derived from drag ballroom culture. These gestures are part of my personal set of cultural references and are meaningful and identifiable to a large swathe of the queer (and ally) community. Each of these moments was inspired by the text, when it created an opening for an emotional, physical response. In these moments I deployed ballroom gestures as a character and as a performer as a way of marking queer territory, and not code switching for a heteronormative population. It's an active choice not to conform.
>
> When I performed these moments in the work, it was empowering and super fun for me, and I hope the audience. These physical choices also helped me let go of some of the neurosis that comes with playing Shakespeare – its history, the gatekeepers involved, the institutional pressures, and expectations of traditionalism – to really focus on character, intention and physicality, which can further illuminate the contemporary relevance of the play. (Bhal, 2022)

It's important to remember that each moment of action is subjectively read and felt. The intersectional effect of the casting worked with and against the incipient demarcations of the sixteenth-century text. Focussing on the lovers in the forest, on the one hand, the fact that there were now three male bodies, more equally matched, diluted the physical violence, which became more comedic. The clowning gestures of men mimicking each other to score points – chasing, ducking and diving – appeared playful when set against the treatment of Hermia within the fight. On the other hand, the diverse casting problematised the potentially racist reading of a particular line. Moosa questioned why when the line 'Away, you Ethiope!'[34] had been cut, replaced by 'Away you ugly bitch', Lysander's exclamation 'Thy love! Out, tawny Tartar, out!' remained; its racial abuse exacerbated when directed at a South Asian female body by a white male.[35] This, alongside a neck-held lift, made the violence of this scene more disturbing. After this, Helenus defends Hermia by punching Lysander in the stomach, delighting Demetrius, who feels his affections are now preferred and who gestures in victory. Moosa felt that the potential for a moment of global majority solidarity, between Demetrius and Helenus, in a shared recognition of

---

[33] Act 3, sc2, line 1337.   [34] Act 3, sc2, line 1299.   [35] Act 3, sc 2, line 1307.

Lysander's racism, had been missed (2021, pp. 61–2). Whilst, to my mind, as a white woman, this redirection would have shifted the intensions of the scene, our differing opinions highlight the nuanced complications of diversifying casting. Our intersectional, relational bodies simultaneously communicate power in a number of ways and bending is always contextual and contingent.

Emma's gender bending casting potential comes into its own in *Wise Children* (2018), which offers an example of *disidentification* in queering. The production was produced in partnership with The Old Vic, adapted by Emma from Angela Carter's final novel about a life in the theatre – a melange of Shakespeare, British thespian families, illegitimacy and incest. She reflects, '*Wise Children* was where it [casting potential] landed, by taking everything I was learning at The Globe and putting it back into my storytelling form' (2022b). The company's inaugural production, previously intended for The Globe, saw seventy-five-year-old twins, Dora and Nora Chance, recount their life story – played at different ages by multiple agents, including the non-human, always with the letters 'D' and 'N' embroidered on their respective tops. As babies and young children, they are played as puppets: as young girls by Mirabelle Gremaud and Bettrys Jones, wearing white dresses with their hair in bunches; as showgirls, by Melissa Jones and male Black actor Omari Douglas, wearing glamorous cabaret costumes; and as the main narrators, played by Gareth Snook and Etta Murfitt, wearing theatrical kimono-style housecoats over their sweaters and skirt/trousers. Emma reflects: 'No two sets of twins were the same. The fact that we were changing generations meant that I could lead the audience to an imaginative space that was both malleable and progressive. *Wise Children* was literally when I shook the rule-book-snow-globe and told the audience 'Come with us! It's going to be OK!' (2022b).

Whilst male to female drag was used in the casting of the twins (Omari Douglas and Gareth Snook), female to male drag was also present, with Patrycja Kujawska multi-rolling as 'the blue-eyed boy' and Lady Atlanta. In its multiplicity, 'naturalising queerness and queering nature' (Braidotti, 2022, p. 160) the casting enables 'queer worldmaking' (Berlant and Warner, 1998).[36] Vicki Mortimer, in conversation with Emma, comments:

> I think your thing about identity is so interesting in *Wise Children*. Essentially it just said, 'I'm going to position these people in these parts and go with it'. Because actually what bubbles up from underneath those casting decisions feels so true to the form of the novel. That you can have Gareth as one of the twins, and you can carry on that complexity and overlapping through all the other roles. And that, in itself, is an expression of the dynamism, and

---

[36] The phrase 'queer world-making' as used by Berlant and Walker describes how queer people create cultures through daily improvisations required by their marginalised statuses.

flexibility of the theatrical making process, that just translated absolutely directly. It solved all those problems about identity in one go. And it was absolutely celebratory from that very core decision. (2020)

In its hopeful celebration of difference and transformation, in the doubling and layering of multiple objects and bodies playing the same role, Braidotti's '"We"-who-are-not-one-and-the-same-but-are-in-*this* together' comes to fruition (Braidotti, 2022, p. 8). The hybridity was inherent in the form, somewhere between a play with songs, musical and cabaret, with constant direct address. The reviews were ecstatic: Kate Kellaway asked 'Stars? I'm not sure why you would stop at five?' (2018b); Arifa Akbar described it as a 'spectacular' evocation of 'the sheer razzle dazzle of a life in the theatre' (2018); and Natasha Tripley called it 'a labour of love if ever there was one' (2018). The Shakespearian matter, paralleling the main storyline, offered countless references to gender fluidity and sexuality. As in *A Midsummer Night's Dream*, this was most directly communicated through the songs, notably a music hall number at the start of the second half, *Girls Will Be Boys When They Want Their Own Way*, with lyrics:

> Whilst we've never had a problem understanding Willi
> His cross-dressing habits were simply overkill
> He dipped his quill in all he fancied
> Hose or Ruff or Quill
> Was he being trans-curious
> Or simply what you will?
> (*Wise Children*, 2020)

The older Nora and Dora remained in role and onstage throughout, whilst the other actors multi-rolled. There were three occasions in the production when all sets of twins were on stage together. The final image saw them all occupying the interior caravan space that had represented their family home, singing Cyndy Laurper's *Girls Just Want to Have Fun*, referencing the novel's original 1980s roots. This image reminded us of an earlier staging, when they all sat in silence, mourning the death of their much-loved Grandma, played with comic aplomb by Katy Owen. The third moment was at the point of anagnorisis in the story, when Dora (Gareth Snook), after sex with her now octogenarian uncle, Pereguine (Mike Shepherd), remembers the abuse she experienced at his hands at thirteen: 'You did me wrong Perry. You stole my childhood. . . . I see more clearly than I've ever seen before'.[37] At this point the ripples of doubling appear in the staging: the old Pereguine sitting centre stage with one bent leg, dressed in the same clothes as the younger Pereguine (Sam Archer), mirroring his position; the older Dora (Etta Murfitt) upstage left, the younger (Bettrys

---

[37] *Wise Children,* adapted by Emma Rice from the novel by Angela Carter. Digital Recording,

Jones) downstage right, replaying the moment when Pereguine removes her pants; and the remaining twins – young Nora (Mirabelle Gremaud) showgirls Nora and Dora (Omari Douglas and Melissa Jones), all witnessing the act. The inevitability of change and transformation was revealed both physically, through the stage picture, reminding us that bodies perform many identities; and psychologically, through staging ripples of memory, lost and found over time – reminding us of our uniquely felt states of becoming different.

If *Wise Children*, with its tale of queer kinship affecting hope and love, is an example of Dolan's theatrical utopia, it did not achieve this through sugar coating and sentimentality. This was a story straddling the pain of humanity – incest, illegitimacy, miscarriage, sexual violence, abuse. Perhaps, in developing her understanding of casting potential, Emma has achieved 'the holy grail', a theatre that, through the power of theatricality, opens up hearts and imaginations to seek a world where it is possible to be anything we want to be, where compassion is available, a theatre of queer worldmaking.

6 Conclusion: Feminist Acts of Love, an Emergent Strategy

respect (n.)
   late 14 c., "relationship, relation; regard, consideration" (as in *in respect to*), from Old French *respect* and directly from Latin *respectus* "regard, a looking at," literally "act of looking back (or often) at one, "noun use of past participle of *respicere*" look back at, regard, consider," from re- "back" (see **re-**) + *specere* "look at" (from PIE root ***spek-** "to observe").[38]

I came to the etymology of the word 'respect' through bell hooks. She makes a connection with the act of looking and seeing beyond 'the mask of categories', to enable mutuality (hooks, 2012, p. 149). This is compelling in relation to theatre. If theatre is a place of seeing, 'looking at' its immediate concern, then how does it conjure respect to enable mutuality? Emma's work asks us to look and then look again; to question whose stories we are telling and who theatre is for? The ethics of affirmativity that underpin her methodology and process (Section 2), ideas of multiplicity and becoming (Section 3) and strategies of queer worldmaking (Section 4) define a practice that seeks a new humanism. Her body of work chases the possibility of freedom and love, infused with hope, bound by respect and working with the positivity of difference (Braidotti, 2022, p. 160). The shared gaze, exchanged between audience and performer, calls for mutual respect – a vulnerable passing between which can engender compassion.

   The dominant theme of Emma's stories is our longing for love in all its messiness and intoxicating pleasure, entwined with pain, driven by hope and

---

[38] Online Etymology Dictionary, www.etymonline.com/word/respect.

desire; all sorts of love – romantic, familial, friendship, love for an animal, love for performance. bell hooks suggests that 'the foundation of all love in our life is the same' it is 'the will to nurture one's own or another's spiritual growth, revealed through acts of care, respect, knowing, and assuming responsibility' (2000 p. 136). I feel this care, respect and nurturing in rehearsal and in performance. It moves me and my body responds: breathing into my belly, my shoulders soften and I smile, opening up to those around me. This shared responsibility, joy and compassion is, I suggest, a type of love.

Central to Black feminist love politics is the need to refigure attitudes to difference. In 1978, June Jordan's talk 'Where is the Love?', at Howard University's national Black writers conference, sparked Black feminists to transform love into a theory of social justice. Three decades later, Jennifer Nash positions Black feminist love politics in the second-wave feminist movement as a way to look beyond the aspects most often associated with Black politics – identity and intersectionality – towards a practice that can transcend limitations of selfhood (2011). Nash problematises the ways that identitarian-focussed institutionalised practice inextricably perpetuates identity categories. She draws on affect theory and the work of Lauren Berlant and Sara Ahmed to ask, 'how do emotions work to align some subjects with some others and against others?' (2011, p. 3). Central to the 'limitations of selfhood' is confronting the fear and anxiety associated with difference. Equally, Audre Lorde insists that we 'reach down into that deep place of knowledge … touch the terror and loathing of any difference that lives there. See whose face it wears. Then the personal as the political can start to illuminate all our choices' (1984 p. 113). Working with and from the positivity of difference is hard work; requiring work on the self in order to be able to work on and with others. Yes, it seeks a utopia, but that doesn't sidestep or pass over the horrors of bodily oppressions. Rather than being seen to be naïve or idealistic, this is a politics that is 'a critical response to the violence of the ordinary and the persistence of inequality that insists on a politics of the visionary' (Nash, 2011 p. 18).

Of course, love isn't a panacea. Sara Ahmed cautions that 'speaking in the name of love' and acting 'out of love' can shut people out as much as it performs an act of seeming generosity and openness. She argues that when indoctrinating groups speak in the name of love, it can be a smokescreen for hate (2003, p.45). Notions of love as a utopian project can easily be part of a humanist fantasy where 'if only we got closer we would be as one'; the flipside of this is that 'those who don't love, who don't get closer, become the source of injury and disturbance' (2003 p. 46). Ahmed isn't dismissing the politics of love, its compunction in the 'intimate "withness" of human relations', she is, however, cautioning that '*how* [my italics] one loves matters' (2003 p. 45).

Turning to Black feminist love politics helps me to think through *how* love operates as a material in Emma's work to produce a radical ethics of care. I recognise that, as she is a white woman, locating her practice in this context could seem misplaced. I fully acknowledge that this feminist movement is contextual and contingent on racism *beside* the position of being woman. However, I see the principles of this activism enacted in Emma's situatedness and enacting through her practice: her minoritarian position in the industry as a woman, an actor/director who hasn't come through the usual university channels; her ideology and the way she has approached certain challenges in her career (Section 1); her methodology and process in rehearsal and on the stage; and what affects happen to individual bodies and to the collective body of the audience (Section 2). This leads me to think about Emma's acts of love in four distinct ways: her own self-respect, remaining true to the work, people and process; extending this care to her company, who then extends it to audiences; creating a sustainable company through the School for Wise Children; and choosing to tell stories that foreground eros – desire and hope.

One of the reasons I was drawn to write about Emma's contribution to theatre was the way she made me feel when I met her. Her generosity, openness and playfulness shine through. Kate Kellaway suggests that Emma is, herself, a 'wise child' (2018a). She has had to make some difficult choices during her career in order to pursue freedom and remain true to herself, her art and ideology – most publicly at The Globe (Section 1). In 1983, Alice Walker proposed that self-love was a prerequisite for the womanist project as without it one could not enable other loves, including pleasure in spirituality, music and dance (Walker, 1983). This position binds the personal and political, where a commitment to well-being and pleasure is, in itself, activism. The T-shirts worn by the Wise Children company in rehearsal, citing Angela Carter, attest to this: 'What a joy it is to dance and sing!' Nourishing others requires self-love.

You could say that Emma, along with her company, are pleasure activists. This doesn't diminish the discipline and rigour of her methodology, the inevitable disagreements and challenges of the creative process. Working with and from 'Joy and Love' (as emblazoned on Etta Murffit's T-shirt) is a prerequisite for creativity, for making boldly vulnerable theatre. As examined in Section 2, this stems from an ethics of affirmativity that speaks to Nash's vision of new forms of community, marked by collective sentiment rather than by identity (2011). In this, individual difference is valued as part of plurality, a quality noted in Emma's ensemble (Cavendish, 2006). The company's collective sentiment – joy and love – is translated on stage and shared with an audience in, what she describes as, 'the human snowball' of affect (2022b). Nash, citing June Jordan, calls for 'a steady state-deep caring and respect for every other human being'

(Jordan qtd in Nash, 2003, p. 272). She suggests that a 'collective public feeling of love' could form the basis of a radical ethic of care. I perceive this in Emma's practice. As Mortimer affirms, her work opens up a world 'where compassion is more available' (2020), and where practicing educated hope is a function of critique.

Wise Children's aims to diversify audiences and practitioners offers theatre an 'emergent strategy', a term used by adrienne maree brown in her ecofeminist activism.[39] In its touring and training remit it is the only UK company to be founded and run by a woman. Kevin Jamieson, Head of Programming at Home Manchester, describes Emma's work as 'quirky and playful, yet also political and thought-provoking' (2018). This popular *and* radical promise, unpacked in Section 1, is inherent in the stories and diverse casting that appeals to medium-scale touring venues around the country. Wise Children works hard to be inclusive and diverse. They invest in Wise Council, an advisory body to help develop audiences, and in digital provision, with all productions available to online audiences from 2020. Their mission statement cites statistics that demarcate acting for the white middle classes through the discriminating cost of training. The School offers free practical, professional development modules and summer schools, led by Emma and members of the company. The company actively seeks new talent, recruiting from local schools and drama groups through outreach workshops. Between 2021 and 2023 they expect to deliver twelve Wise Children training modules, reaching 150 trainees. They state:

> This area of our work is crucial. It will create a more diverse artistic workforce, who will produce theatre which tells stories from all parts of our society. It will ensure that people from all communities and backgrounds are represented both on stage and behind the scenes. In turn, this will help to attract more diverse audiences, creating work which appeals to all.[40]

This commitment to the positivity of difference could be seen as, citing bell hooks, an example of 'radical openness' (1989).

Rosi Braidotti argues that, in order for humans to look beyond the mechanisms of advanced capitalism, eros needs to enter the posthuman equation (2022, p. 206). With a more generous and expansive conception of love, love activism can deterritorialise, reorder and reshape systems of control. Desire and the condition of hope are forward motions, a moving horizon, stretching ahead, asking, 'What if'? I feel this affect in Emma's work as lovers defy gravity, bird-like, swinging from chandeliers, ecstatically soaring and swooping, reaching out, beyond the audience, between the no longer and the not yet.

---

[39] *Emergent Strategy: Shaping Change, Changing Worlds* (AK Press, Scotland: 2017).

[40] *Wise Children* Mission Statement – shared in email exchange with Helen Comerford.

What if? What if? What if?

It gives me goosebumps, not because I am intoxicated by love, but because hopeful liberation makes me feel alive, connected, compassionate. In that forward movement I am reminded of hooks' assertion: 'The moment we choose to love, we begin to move toward freedom, to act in ways that liberate ourselves and others' (2000, p. 158). Emma's feminist acts of love, her insistence on freedom, mutuality and hope performs an emergent strategy for theatre and beyond – inviting us to flock, in mutual synchronicity, towards a new humanism.

Appendix

The Itch – Kneehigh, UK, 1999

The Red Shoes – Kneehigh, UK tour 2000–2, and US and Australia 2010–11. Winner of TMA best director 2002

Pandora's Box – Kneehigh, UK tour 2002

The Wooden Frock – Kneehigh, UK tour 2003–4. Nominated for TMA best touring production 2004

The Bacchae – Kneehigh, UK tour, 2005 (Section 5)

Nights at the Circus – Kneehigh, UK, Lyric Hammersmith and Bristol Old Vic, 2005

Tristan and Yseult – Kneehigh, National Theatre, UK 2006, 2013 and US 2013–2015 (Section 4)

Rapunzel – Kneehigh, UK tour, 2007, 2010

Cymbeline – Kneehigh, UK 2006 and New York, 2007–8

A Matter of Life and Death – National Theatre, 2007

Don John – Kneehigh/RSC, UK tour, 2008–9 (Section 4)

The Umbrellas of Cherbourg – Kneehigh, Gielgud Theatre, 2011

Steptoe and Son – Kneehigh, UK tour, 2012–13

Oedipussy – SpyMonkey, UK tour 2012

Brief Encounter – Kneehigh, UK/USA 2009, Broadway 2010, Australia and US 2013–14

The Wild Bride – Kneehigh, UK, New York, New Zealand, 2011–13 (Section 4)

Wah! Wah! Girls – Sadlers Wells, 2012

Midnight's Pumpkin – Kneehigh, Battersea Arts Centre, 2012

The Empress – RSC, 2013

Rebecca – Kneehigh/David Pugh, UK tour, 2015

946: The Amazing Story of Adolphus Tips – Kneehigh, UK and US, 2016

The Flying Lovers of Vitesbsk – Kneehigh, Shakespeare's Globe, 2016

A Midsummer Night's Dream – Shakespeare's Globe, 2016 (Section 5)

The Little Matchgirl – Shakespeare's Globe, 2016 and UK tour

Romantics Anonymous – Shakespeare's Globe, 2017, Bristol Old Vic, 2020

The Little Match Girl – Shakespeare's Globe, 2017

Twelfth Night – Shakespeare's Globe, 2017

Wise Children – Wise Children, Old Vic, 2018 (Section 5)

Orpheus in the Underworld – English National Opera, 2019

Mallory Towers – Wise Children/David Pugh, 2019

Bagdad Café – Wise Children, Old Vic, 2021

Wuthering Heights – Wise Children, UK and US, 2021–2

References

Ahmed, S. (2003). 'In the Name of Love', *Borderlands e-journal*, 2(3). www
.borderlands.net.au/vol2no3_2003?ahmed_love.htm (accessed 10 June
2017)

Akbar, A. (2010). 'Mallory Towers Review – Emma Rice Takes Blyton to the
Top of the Class'. *The Guardian*, 26 June. www.theguardian.com/stage/
2019/jul/26/malory-towers-review-emma-rice-enid-blyton-passenger-
shed-bristol (accessed 25 August 2022)

(2018). 'Wise Children Review – Emma Rice's Spectacular Angela Carter
Carnival'. *The Guardian*, 19 October. www.theguardian.com/stage/2018/
oct/19/wise-children-review-emma-rice-angela-carter-old-vic-london
(accessed 12 August 2022)

Aston, E. (2020). *Restaging Feminisms* (Palgrave Macmillan, London)

(1995). *An Introduction to Feminism and Theatre* (Routledge, London)

Aston, E., and Harris, G. (2015). *A Good Night out For The Girls: Popular
Feminisms in Contemporary Theatre and Performance* (Palgrave
Macmillan, London)

Arendt, H. (1998). *The Human Condition* (University of Chicago Press, Chicago,
Illinois)

Barad, K. (2003). 'Posthumanist Performativity: Towards an Understanding of
How Matter Comes to Matter', *Signs*, 28(3), 801–31

Babbage, F. (2018). *Adaptation in Contemporary Theatre: Performing
Literature* (Methuen Drama, Bloomsbury, London)

Bennet, J. (2010). *Vibrant Matter: A Political Ecology of Things* (Duke
University Press, Durham, North Carolina)

De Beauvoir, S. (1997). *The Second Sex* (Vintage Books, London)

Berlant, L., and Warner, M. (1998). 'Sex in Public', *Critical Inquiry, Intimacy*
24(2), 547–66

Billington, M. (2009). 'Don't Let Auteurs Take over in Theatre'. *The
Guardian*, 14 April. www.guardian.co.uk/stage/theatreblog/2009/apr/
14/auteur- (accessed 16 July 2011)

(2008). 'Don John'. *The Guardian*, 20 December. www.theguardian.com/
stage/2008/dec/20/kneehigh-don-john-review (accessed 12 August 2022)

Bowes, S. (2019). 'Notes towards a Theatre of Assemblages', *Performance
Research*, 24(4), 28–34

Bhebhe, N. (2022). Interview with Author, Brighton, 18 May

Bhal, A. (2022). Interview with the Author via Zoom, 10 October

Braidotti, R. (2022). *Posthuman Feminism* (Polity Press, Cambridge)

(2011). *Nomadic Theory: The Portable Rosi Braidotti* (Columbia University Press, New York)

Braidotti, R. (2001). *Metamorphoses: Towards and Materialist Theory of Becoming* (Polity Press, Cambridge)

Brown, A. M. (2017). *Emergent Strategy: Shaping Change, Changing Worlds* (AK Press, California)

Butler, J. (2015). *Notes toward a Performative Theory of Assembly* (Harvard University Press, Cambridge, Massachusetts)

(2006). *Gender Trouble.* (Routledge, London)

(1993). *Bodies that Matter: On the Discursive Limits of Sex* (Routledge, London)

Case, S. E. (1990). *Performing Feminisms: Feminist Critical Theory and Theatre* (John Hopkins University Press, Baltimore, Maryland)

(1998). *Feminism in Theatre* (Routledge, New York)

Cavendish, D. (2018). 'Wise Children at The Old Vic, SE1'. *The Times*, 19 April. www.thetimes.co.uk/article/theatre-review-wise-children-at-the-old-vic-se1-xdsjm2f9d (accessed 15 April 2020)

(2006). 'A Shot in the Arm for the Junkie King'. *The Telegraph*, 26 September. www.telegraph.co.uk/culture/theatre/drama/3655572/A-shot-in-the-arm-from-the-junkie-king.html (accessed 1 June 2015)

Cixous, H. (1976). 'The Laugh of the Medusa', *Signs*, 1(4), 875–93

Clapp, S. (2016). 'A Midsummer Night's Dream Review – The Wildest of Dreams'. *The Guardian*, 8 May. www.theguardian.com/stage/2016/may/08/midsummer-nights-dream-shakespeares-globe-theatre-review-emma-rice (accessed 21 June 2022)

Costa, M. (2015). 'Troupe Therapy'. *The Guardian*. 1 December. www.theguardian.com/stage/2008/dec/01/kneehigh-theatre-cornwall-maddy-costa (accessed 8 February 2016)

Dale, M. (2022). 'Britain's National Theatre Director Rufus Norris Commits to Fifty-Fifty Gender Balance by 2021'. *Broadway World*, 4 February. www.broadwayworld.com/article/Britains-National-Theatre-Director-Rufus-Norris-Commits-To-5050-Gender-Balance-By-2021-20160204 (accessed 9 September 2022)

DeLanda, M. (2016). *Assemblage Theory* (University of Edinburgh Press, Edinburgh)

Deleuze, G. (2005). *Pure Imminence: Essays on a Life* (Princetown University Press, New Jersey)

Deleuze, G., and Guattari, F. (1987). *A Thousand Plateaus: Capitalism and Schizophrenia* (University of Minnesota Press, Minneapolis, Minnesota)

Deleuze, G., and Parnet, C. (2007). *Dialogues II* (Columbia University Press, New York)

Diamond, E. (1997). *Unmaking Mimesis* (Routledge, London)

Dolan, J. (2005). *Utopia in Performance: Finding Hope at the Theatre* (University of Michigan Press, Ann Arbor, Michigan)

(1988). *The Feminist Spectator as Critic* (University of Michigan Press, Ann Arbor, Michigan)

Furness, H. (2017). 'Shakespeare's Globe Advertises for New Director with Passion for Its Past after Row over Modern Lighting'. *The Telegraph*, 27 March. www.telegraph.co.uk/news/2017/03/27/shakespeares-globe-advertises-new-director-passion-past-row/ (accessed 22 June 2022)

Freud, S. (2018). *Three Essays on the Theory of Sexuality* (StreetLib Write)

Gale, D. (2021). 'Kneehigh Theatre to Close after "Changes in Artistic Leadership"'. *The Guardian*, 3 June. www.theguardian.com/stage/2021/jun/03/kneehigh-theatre-close-changes-artistic-leadership#:~:text=The%20award-winning%20Kneehigh%20theatre,a (accessed 13 September 2022)

Gardner, L. (2021). 'Emma Rice: Directing Theatre and Being Fearless', *Digital Theatre Plus*. https://edu-digitaltheatreplus-com.ezproxy.sussex.ac.uk/content/guides/emma-rice-directing-theatre-and-being-fearless (accessed 7 July 2022)

(2016a). 'It's Time for a Big Adventure: Emma Rice on Her Opening Globe Production'. *The Guardian*, 11 April. www.theguardian.com/stage/2016/apr/11/emma-rice-interview-shakespeares-globe-theatre-wonder-season-midsummer-nights-dream (accessed 16 July 2022)

(2016b). 'As Emma Rice Departs, The Globe Has Egg on Its Face – and No Vision'. *The Guardian*, 25 September. www.theguardian.com/stage/theatreblog/2016/oct/25/shakespeares-globe-emma-rice-department-comment (accessed 6 July 2022)

(2022). 'The Wild Bride Review'. *The Guardian*, 13 September. www.theguardian.com/stage/2011/sep/13/wild-bride-hammersmith-review (accessed 12 July 2022)

Gatens, M. (1996). *Imaginary Bodies: Ethics, Power and Corporality* (Routledge, London)

Gregg, M., and Seigworth, G. (2010). *The Affect Theory Reader* (Duke University Press, Durham, North Carolina)

Grosz, E. (1994). *Volatile Bodies: Towards a Corporeal Feminism* (Indiana University Press, : Bloomington, Indiana)

Haraway, D. (2016). *Staying with the Trouble: Making Kin in the Chthulucene* (Duke University Press, Durham, North Carolina)

(2003). *The Companion Species Manifesto: Dogs, People and Significant Otherness* (Prickly Paradigm Press, Chicago)

Heath, S. (1985). 'Joan Riviere and The Masquerade' In *Formations of Fantasy*, eds Burgin, V., Donald, J., and Kaplan, C. (London: Routledge)

Heller, M. (2020). *Queering Drag: Redefining the Discourse of Gender Bending* (Indiana University Press, Bloomington, Indiana)

Hemming, S. (2019). 'National Theatre Director Rufus Norris on Andrea Levy's Small Island'. *Financial Times*, 19 April. www.ft.com/content/07a0e408-5f9e-11e9-9300-0becfc937c37 (accessed 16 September 2022)

Hooks, B. (2012). *Writing beyond Race: Living Theory and Practice* (Taylor and Francis Group, Oxforshire)

(2010). *Teaching Critical Thinking Practical Wisdom* (Routledge, London)

(2000). *All about Love* (Harper Perennial, London)

(1989). 'Choosing the Margin as a Space for Radical Openness', *Framework: The Journal of Cinema and Media*, 36, 15–23

Hoyle, B. (2007). 'Dead White Me in the Critics Chair Scorning the Work of Women Directors'. *The Times*, 14 May. www.thetimes.co.uk/article/dead-white-men-in-the-critics-chair-scorning-work-of-women-directors-6jn7025295h (accessed 6 August 2022)

Hurley, E. (2010). *Theatre and Feeling* (Methuen, Bloomsbury, London)

Irigaray, L. (1985). *This Sex Which is Not One* (Cornell University Press, New York)

Jamieson, K. (2018). *Wise Children* Mission Statement – Shared with Helen Comerford in an Email Exchange.

Jordan, J. (2003). *Some of Us Did Not Die* (Basic Books, New York)

Johnson, C. (2022). Interview with the Author, Brighton, 21 May

Kellaway, K. (2018a). 'Emma Rice: I Don't Know How I Got to be So Controversial'. *Observer*, 1 July. www.theguardian.com/stage/2018/jul/01/emma-rice-controversial-shakespeares-globe-wise-children (accessed 5 August 2022)

(2018b). 'Wise Children Review – Emma Rice's Joyous Angela Carter Adaptation'. *The Guardian*, 21 October. www.theguardian.com/stage/2018/oct/21/wise-children-old-vic-review-emma-rice-angela-carter (accessed 13 August 2022)

Kujawska, P. (2022a). Interviewed by the Author, Somerset, 21 July

(2022b). Interviewed by the Author on Zoom, 6 July

Lacan, J. (1949). 'Mirror Stage as Formative of the *I* Function, as Revealed in Psychoanalytical Experience'. In *Ecrits: A Selection*, trans. Fink, B., pp. 75–82. (New York: W.W. Norton)

Lempiäinen, K. (2010). 'With You but Different: Jouissance and Feminist Writing', *Nordic Journal of Women's Studies*, 5(2), 105–18.

Letts, Q. (2018). 'Bonkers but Brilliant, a Very English Rice Pudding: Quentin Letts Reviews Wise Children at the Old Vic'. *Daily Mail*, 19 September. www.dailymail.co.uk/tvshowbiz/article-6292981/QUENTIN-LETTS-reviews-Wise-Children-Old-Vic.html (accessed 16 June 2022)

Lorde, A. (2017). 'Age, Race, Class and Sex: Women Redefining Difference' in *Your Silence Will Not Protect You*, (Silver Press)

(1984). *Sister Outsider* (Crossing Press, Berkley)

Maltby, K. (2016). 'Emma Rice Was Never as Radical as She Thought She Was'. *The Spectator*, 26 October. www.spectator.co.uk/article/emma-rice-was-never-as-radical-as-she-thought-she-was (accessed 13 August 2022)

McCormick, L. (2022). Interview with the Author via Zoom, 23 May

Moosa, H. (2021). 'Review of Shakespeare's A Midsummer Night's Dream', *Shakespeare*, 17(1), 58–63

Morrison, R. (2016). 'The Globe Has Been a Success Story and Emma Rice is Wrecking It'. *The Times*, 30 September. www.thetimes.co.uk/article/rich ard-morrison-the-globe-has-been-a-success-story-and-emma-rice-is-wrecking-it-xrrgxz3ml (accessed 20 September 2022)

Mortimer, V. (2020). 'Tea and Biscuits with Emma Rice'. *Wise Children Podcast*, 11 June. https://podcastaddict.com/podcast/2980147 (accessed 16 July 2022)

Nash, J. (2011). 'Practicing Love: Black Feminism, Love-Politics, and Post-Intersectionality', *Meridians*, 11(2), 1–24

Owen, K. (2022). Interview with Author, Brighton, 18 May

Peck, L. (2021). *Act as a Feminist: Towards a Critical Acting Pedagogy* (Routledge, London)

Phelan, P. (1993). *Unmarked: The Politics of Performance* (Routledge, London)

Price, J. (2016). *Modern Popular Theatre* (Palgrave Macmillan, London)

Radosavljević, D. (2013a). *The Contemporary Ensemble: Interviews with Theatre-Makers* (Routledge, London)

(2013b). *Theatre-Making: Interplay between Text and Performance in the 21st Century* (Palgrave Macmillan, London)

Rice, E. (2022a). Interviewed by the Author via Zoom, 16 August

(2022b). Interview with Author on Zoom, 30 August

(2016). Interviewed by Kerbel, L., 'What's on Stage: Tonic Theatre: Emma Rice', 21 October. www.facebook.com/whatsonstage/videos/tonic-cele brates-emma-rice/10153865037575896/ (accessed 17 December 2022)

(2020). In Conversation with Kujawska, P., 'Tea and Biscuits' Podcast for Wise Children. www.wisechildrendigital.com/_files/ugd/f32126_36589dd 75ebc4cc5ac8a4fa542cc8d66.pdf (accessed 20 July 2022)

(2016). Programme note *A Midsummer Night's Dream*, The Globe.

(2015). Interviewed by the Author in Bristol, 29 January

Riviere, J. (1986). 'Womanliness as a Masquerade'. In *Formations of Fantasy*, eds. Burgin, V., Donald, J., and Kaplan, C. (Routledge, London)

Rogers, J. (2019). 'Cross-Cultural Casting in Britain: The Path to Inclusion 1972–2012'. *Multicultural Shakespeare*, 19(1), 55–70

Ross, I . (2022) Interviewed by the Author, Oxford, 29th July

Sedgwick, E. (2003). *Touching Feeling: Affect, Pedagogy, Performativity* (Duke University Press, Durham)

Shakespeare, W. *A Midsummer Night's Dream*, Open Source Shakespeare www .opensourceshakespeare.org/views/plays/play_view.php?WorkID=mid summer&Act=3&Scene=1&Scope=scene (accessed 12 January 2022)

Singh, A. (2017). 'Come and Work at Shakespeare's Globe – If You Can Put Up With the Cabals, the Connivers and the Personality Problems'. *The Telegraph*, 19 April. www.telegraph.co.uk/news/2017/04/19/come-work-shakespeares-globe-can-put-cabals-connivers-personality/ (accessed 22 April 2017)

Spinoza, B. (1996). *Ethics* (Penguin Books, New York)

Simpson, R. (2022). 'Brief Encounter – Stephen Joseph Theatre, Scarborough'. *TheReviewsHub*, 27 July. www.thereviewshub.com/brief-encounter-ste phen-joseph-theatre-scarborough/ (accessed 3 July 2022)

Smith, B. (2016). 'Queer Goings On', Programme note *A Midsummer Night's Dream*, The Globe

Solga, K. (2016). *Theatre and Feminism* (Palgrave Macmillan, London)

Spatz, B. (2015). *What a Body Can Do: Technique as Knowledge, Practice as Research* (Routledge, London)

Spivak, G. (1988). 'Can the Subaltern Speak?'. In *Marxism and the Interpretation of Culture*, eds. Nelson, C., and Grossberg, L., pp. 271–313. (Macmillan Education, Basingstoke)

Staff writers, (2007). 'Are the Critics Strangling Theatre'. *The Guardian*, 15 May. www.theguardian.com/stage/2007/may/15/theatre3 (accessed 12 July 2022)

Staff writers, (2002). 'Obituary. Theatre's Defiant Genius'. *BBC News*, 21 September. http://news.bbc.co.uk/1/hi/uk/1628351.stm (accessed 16 February 2013)

Stamatiou, E. (2020). 'Inclusive Casting Debunked: Towards Holistic Interventions in Staged Performance', *Interdisciplinary Perspectives on Equality and Diversity*, 6(2), 1–31

Sturrock, T. (2022). Interview with Author, Somerset, 21 July

Thompson, A. (2006). *Colorblind Shakespeare: New Perspectives on Race and Performance* (Routledge, London)

Tomlin, L. (2015). *British Theatre Companies 1995–2014* (Bloomsbury, London)

Trenchfield, C. (2022). *The Global and Local Appeal of Kneehigh Theatre Company* (Cambridge Scholars, UK)

Tripley, N. (2018). 'Wise Children'. *The Stage*, 19 October. www.thestage.co .uk/reviews/wise-children-review-at-old-vic-london–mess-melancholy- and-magic (accessed 8 August 2022)

Walker, A. (1983). *In Search of Our Mothers' Gardens* (Harcourt Brace, New York)

Wandor, M. (1986). *Carry on Understudies: Theatre and Sexual Politics* (Routledge, London)

Watson, I. (2004). Bacchae Review, *What's On Stage*. Accessed in Falmouth archive (8 September 2022)

Acknowledgements

This Element would not have been possible without the generous support and enthusiasm of Emma Rice and all at Wise Children: Helen Comerford for her patience, responsiveness and exceptional organisation skills; Simon Baker for his brilliant help with accessing productions; Poppy Keeling, Rhys Bugler, Steph Curtis and Laura Keefe for friendly field-work support. Thanks to interviewees: Craig Johnson, Katy Owen, Nandi Bhebhe, Lucy McCormack, Patrycja Kujawska, Tristan Sturrock, Ankur Bahl and Ian Ross. Thanks to Steve Tanner and Leah Gordon for the images. To all those shiny, talented artists in rehearsal for *Blue Beard*, The Wise Children Summer School and *The Buddha of Suburbia* – thanks for inviting me in to play. And of course, thanks to Emma for the work, her time, openness, hospitality and indominable spirit. It has been a joy.

I would like to thank Elaine Aston for the invitation to submit to the series. Thanks to The University of Sussex for giving me study leave between July 2022 and January 2023 to work on this project; to colleagues, particularly Augusto Corrieri for conversations about writing. Thanks to Rowena and Carol at Falmouth Archive for their enthusiasm and support. Thanks to Catherine Trenchfield for generously sharing her research. Special thanks to Duska Radosavljevic for her inspirational work and invaluable feedback on this manuscript.

Thanks to mum and dad for hosting me in a writing retreat. To my dear friends, Gill, Jas, KP and Genevieve who give me courage and keep me moving forward. To my family, Simon, Ella, Olive and Isobel. Every day you all teach me how to love better.

Love is the answer.

Cambridge Elements ≡

Women Theatre Makers

Elaine Aston
Lancaster University

Elaine Aston is internationally acclaimed for her feminism and theatre research. Her monographs include *Caryl Churchill* (1997); *Feminism and Theatre* (1995); *Feminist Theatre Practice* (1999); *Feminist Views on the English Stage* (2003); and *Restaging Feminisms* (2020). She has served as Senior Editor of Theatre Research International (2010–12) and President of the International Federation for Theatre Research (2019–23).

Melissa Sihra
Trinity College Dublin

Melissa Sihra is Associate Professor in Drama and Theatre Studies at Trinity College Dublin. She is author of *Marina Carr: Pastures of the Unknown* (2018) and editor of *Women in Irish Drama: A Century of Authorship and Representation* (2007). She was President of the Irish Society for Theatre Research (2011–15) and is currently researching a feminist historiography of the Irish playwright and co-founder of the Abbey Theatre, Lady Augusta Gregory.

Advisory Board

Nobuko Anan, *Kansai University, Japan*
Awo Mana Asiedu, *University of Ghana*
Ana Bernstein, *UNIRIO, Brazil*
Elin Diamond, *Rutgers, USA*
Bishnupriya Dutt, *JNU, India*
Penny Farfan, *University of Calgary, Canada*
Lesley Ferris, *Ohio State University, USA*
Lisa FitzPatrick, *University of Ulster, Northern Ireland*
Lynette Goddard, *Royal Holloway, University of London, UK*
Sarah Gorman, *Roehampton University, UK*
Aoife Monks, *Queen Mary, London University, UK*
Kim Solga, *Western University, Canada*
Denise Varney, *University of Melbourne, Australia*

About the Series

This innovative, inclusive series showcases women-identifying theatre makers from around the world. Expansive in chronological and geographical scope, the series encompasses practitioners from the late nineteenth century onwards and addresses a global, comprehensive range of creatives – from playwrights and performers to directors and designers.

Cambridge Elements ≡

Women Theatre Makers

Printed in the United States
by Baker & Taylor Publisher Services